A WORKBOOK FOR READERS
A Basic Course for Readers

A supplement to
A Handbook for Readers:
a practical and liturgical guide

Marian Tolley

Decani Books

First published in 2004 by Decani Music Ltd, Oak House, 70 High Street, Brandon, Suffolk IP27 0AU

ISBN 1 900314 14 2

Printed by RPM Print & Design Ltd, Units 2-3 Spur Road, Quarry Lane, Chichester, West Sussex, PO19 8PR

Acknowledgements

Scripture texts taken from *The Jerusalem Bible*, published and copyright 1966, 1967 and 1968 by Darton, Longman and Todd Ltd, and used by permission of the publishers..

Psalm texts from *The Psalms: A New Translation*, translated from the Hebrew by the Grail. Published by HarperCollins. © 1963 The Grail (England). Used by permssion of HarperCollins.

Excerpt from *Reading the Gospels with the Church from Christmas through Easter,* by Raymond E Brown, SS, ©1996 St Anthony Messenger Press. Used by permission. All rights reserved.

Excerpt from *Sharing the Lectionary for Lent 2002: a Participant's Handbook* © 2001 Resource Publications , Inc., 160 E. Virginia Street, #290 San Jose, CA 95112-5876 www.rpinet.com. Used by permission. All rights reserved.

Excerpts from *Word and Worship Workbook Year A* by Mary Birmingham © 1999 Paulist Press, Inc, New York/Mahwah, N.J. Used with permission of Paulist Press. www.paulistpress.com

Excerpts from *Let the Scriptures Speak* by Dennis Hamm, © 2001 Liturgical Press, Collegeville, Minnesota, and *The Cultural World of Jesus, Cycle A,* by John J Pilch, © 1995 The Liturgical Press. Used by permission. All rights reserved.

Excerpts from *A Workbook for Lectors and Gospel Readers* by Aelred Rosser, © 2002 Liturgy Training Publications, and from *A Workbook for Lectors: A Well-Trained Tongue* by Ray Longergan, © 1982 Liturgy Training Publications. Used by permission. All rights reserved.

Excerpts from the English translation of the *General Introduction to the Lectionary for Mass* © 1969, 1981, International Committee on English in the Liturgy, Inc. and from the *Constitution on the Liturgy from Documents on the Liturgy, 1968-1979: Conciliar, Papal and Curial Texts,* © 1982 ICEL. All rights reserved.

CONTENTS

Before we begin   5

Introduction

   1. Statements about liturgy   6

   2. Basic assumptions   5

Part One: General Background

A. Church Documents

   Extracts from *The General Introduction to the Lectionary*   8

B. The Bible

   1. Introductory note   13

   2. The Books of the Old Testament   14

   3. The Books of the New Testament   20

C. From Bible to Lectionary   21

Part Two: Improving Proclamation

A. Reflection   23

   1. Begin preparation early

   2. Listening and telling

   3. Read the passage aloud

   4. Pray with the text

B. Research   24

   5. Check correct pronunciation of place and proper names

   6. Read the passage in its proper context in the scriptures

   7. Study scripture commentaries

   8. Find answers to questions raised by the text

C. Rehearsal   26

   9. Make use of basic communication skills

   10. Practise with the microphone

   11. Get help: ask a friend to listen critically

D. Review   29

12. Evaluate your interpretations and delivery
13. Get a trusted friend to provide a critique

E. Special situations

1. The Psalms especially when not sung   30
2. Preparing a reading from Paul's writings   34
3. The Book of Revelation   37

Part Three – Ministry   40

Appendices

A. Current Order of Readings   44

B. Exercises useful in preparation of scriptural texts   49

C. Samples of scripture commentaries   59

Reading List   70

Footnotes   72

Before We Begin

THIS WORKBOOK arises from a desire to provide in one place a comprehensive selection of materials which will help people who read Scripture in worship.

My experience of conducting courses for readers in the Diocese of Wrexham suggests that not everyone involved in this ministry has access to the documentation, nor can their parishes provide the range of material which will enable them to identify and work on aspects of public speech. There are some excellent resources available, but it is not likely that either individuals or parishes will be able to invest in the full range.

Hence this Workbook.

It contains extracts from the relevant official documents, practical exercises for readers, and samples of resources such as scripture commentaries which are useful in preparation and which readers can decide to go on and buy for themselves. In this way, the Workbook is an anthology suggesting further reading and study. The material has been developed through use in workshops with readers and is recommended for individual and group work in parishes.

As I have been assembling these materials it has become evident to me that careful preparation of the proclamation of the Word will be increasingly important as many parishes find themselves unable to celebrate Mass on Sunday because no priest is available. In many such circumstances, the community will hold a liturgy of Word and Communion, when it will be even more imperative that the Word be carefully prepared and powerfully delivered.

Introduction

■ 1. Statements about Liturgy

The place to begin is with the importance of liturgy – public worship – because the role that readers fill is an essential part of that worship. It is viial that all who worship together have the understanding of the importance of liturgy which is expressed very clearly in the following direct quotations from the Constitution on the Sacred Liturgy (*CSL*). Emphasis has been added and paragraph numbers are in brackets.

The *CSL* says that liturgy is:

a. the **outstanding means** whereby the faithful may express in their lives and manifest to others the mystery of Christ and the real nature of the true Church. [2]

b. an exercise of the priestly office of Christ [7]

c. a foretaste of that heavenly liturgy celebrated in the holy city of Jerusalem. [7]

d. a sacred action **surpassing all others, no other action of the Church can equal its effectiveness** by the same title and to the same degree…[7]

e. the **summit** toward which the activity of the Church is directed; at the same time it is the **fount from which** all the Church's power flows…[10]

f. the source for achieving in **the most effective way possible** human sanctification and God's glorification, the end to which all the Church's other activities are directed…[10]

g. 'The Church earnestly desires that all the faithful be led to that **full, conscious, and active participation** in liturgical celebration…

   called for **by the very nature of the liturgy,**

   such participation by the Christian people…is **their right and duty** by reason of their baptism.

   this full and active participation by all the people is **the aim to be considered before all else**. For it is **the primary and indispensable source** from which the faithful are to derive the true Christian spirit…'[14]

It is worth taking some time to ponder these statements (the best way is to read them aloud with the suggested emphasis) and to return to them regularly. The unequivocal power and clarity of their expression needs to be at the heart of our understanding of what we do when we come together for liturgy. This is true especially for those who are involved in the proclamation of the Word. The constant awareness of the importance of liturgy will remind us of how awesome and wonderful is the responsibility of giving voice to the Word of God.

2. Basic Assumptions

a. 'Liturgy' is *public* worship (as distinct from private prayer). It is characterised by a ritual format which includes the use of scripture, symbol, and music. The summit of liturgy is the Suâday Eucharist – it is the occasion when the greatest number of us gathers because we have been called to celebrate the passion, death and resurrection of Christ in remembrance of him. While Sunday Mass is not the only form of liturgy, it is the pre-eminent one. In what follows, 'liturgy' will refer solely to the Sunday celebration.

b. **Liturgy matters.** This is borne out in all of the statements given above, but it must also be the conviction of those with a ministry during Mass, especially readers for whom this Workbook is assembled.

c. **Good liturgy does not happen by accident.** There are many elements in the Sunday celebration – ministers, symbols, music, environment – and all of them need attention if worship is to be given its proper value. This means that rehearsal is useful, even essential because it is the best way of ensuring that everyone is aware of all aspects of their ministry, comfortable with them, and aware of how they fit with the roles of other ministers. Good preparation is at least half of what is needed for good liturgy; time for evaluation afterwards is also important.

d. **We are not starting from scratch.** There is much good practice already in place. Those involved in the ministry of reading have volunteered because they wish to be of service to their community, and they wish to do their work well. This Workbook is designed to act as a support and a reference to help those already doing good work: to refresh their understanding and improve their skills.

e. **What is the purpose of the Liturgy of the Word?**

In all of our making ready to proclaim the Word of God, it is helpful to remember that '…the liturgy of the word is **a dialogue between God and the assembled community.**'[1] God speaks to his people in the First and Second Readings, the Psalm and the Gospel; his people respond in the Psalm, sing to welcome the Gospel, proclaim their Faith and offer prayers of intercession.

f. **There is always room for improvement.** We should consider what St Benedict wrote about readers of scripture in his Rule fifteen hundred years ago:

'They should not presume to read who by mere chance take up the book…. Only those are to discharge these duties who can do so to the edification of the heavens.'

PART ONE:
General Background

Contents of Part One: A: Church Documents;
B: The Bible (p.14); C: From Bible to Lectionary (p.21)

A. Church Documents bearing on the Liturgy of the Word

Extracts from *The General Introduction to the Lectionary*

There are two books which are used during the celebration of the Mass; together they are called *The Roman Missal.* The two parts are –

The Sacramentary*:* the altar Missal containing all the prayers said by the priest and people during Mass.

The Lectionary: the extracts taken from books of the Bible organised for use during Mass throughout the liturgical year.

Both have Introductions, The General Instruction of the Roman Missal (GIRM), and The General Introduction to the Lectionary (GIL) which explain everything they contain, not only *what* each part of the Mass is and *how* it should be done, but also *why* the rites are as they are. Both Introductions are highly recommended to be read in their entirety.

The General Introduction to the Lectionary is the most valuable guide to readers of scripture. For this reason, it is quoted extensively here to put in the hands of readers the most helpful information.

▪ 1. What is *The General Introduction to the Lectionary?*

The revised Lectionary was introduced in 1969 and was among the first fruits of the 2nd Vatican Council. A second edition in 1981 made few changes to the scriptural texts, but had a greatly expanded introduction which provides the following:

- An explanation of the close relationship between the word of God and the liturgical celebration and what is going on during the Liturgy of the Word.
- A list of all those with ministerial responsibility during the Liturgy of the Word, and an outline of their responsibilities.
- An explanation of the structure of the Order of Readings for the Mass.

2. Highlights of the *General Introduction to the Lectionary*

[N.B. emphasis – italics and bold type – has been added by the author.]

2a. What is going on during the Liturgy of the Word?

Christ is present in his word; as he carries out the mystery of salvation, he sanctifies us and offers the Father perfect worship. [4]

That word constantly proclaimed in the liturgy is always...a living, active word *through the power of the Holy Spirit.* [4]

Whenever, therefore, the Church, gathered by the Holy Spirit for liturgical celebration, announces and proclaims the word of God, **it has the experience of being a new people in whom the *covenant made in the past is fulfilled*.** [7]

...it is from the word of God handed down in writing that even now **'*God is speaking to his people*....**[12]

For the reader and for everyone present at the liturgy, these statements should help us understand that the Liturgy of the Word is not something passive, but an occasion of active dialogue when God's work is alive and we participate as receivers of his promise. This requires all of us to be alert and ready to hear the message.

2b. What is the relationship between the Liturgy of the Word and the Liturgy of the Eucharist?

The Liturgy of the Word and the Liturgy of the Eucharist are the two main components of the Mass: they are both essential and indissolubly linked. The *GIL* states clearly how they are related:

The Church is nourished spiritually at the table of God's word and at the table of the eucharist: from the one it grows in wisdom and from the other in holiness. In the word of God the divine covenant is announced; in the eucharist the new and everlasting covenant is renewed. The spoken word of God brings to mind the history of salvation; the eucharist embodies it in the sacramental signs of the liturgy. [10]

2c. What are the elements of the Liturgy of the Word?

• Biblical readings

The first reading is from the Old Testament, the second from an apostle (either a letter or from Revelation, depending on the season), and the third from the gospel. [66.1] The gospel is the high point: for this the other readings prepare the assembly. [13]

• The Responsorial Psalm

As a rule, the responsorial psalm should be sung. [20]

To foster the congregation's singing...use is to be made of all the relevant options provided in the Order of Readings for Mass. [21]

To make it easier for the people to join in the response to the psalm, the Order of Readings lists certain other texts of psalms and responses that have been chosen according to the various seasons.... Whenever the psalm is sung, these texts may replace the text corresponding to the reading. [89]

When not sung, the psalm after the reading is to be recited in a manner conducive to meditation on the word of God.

The responsorial psalm is sung or recited by the psalmist or cantor at the lectern. [22]

It is important to emphasise here that if the psalm is not sung, it is to be treated in the same manner as the other scriptural texts in the liturgy. That is, the same preparation and care in proclamation outlined later are to be applied to the proclamation of the psalm text. See below, page 31.

• Acclamation before the reading of the Gospel

The Alleluia, or, as the liturgical season requires, the verse before the gospel...serves as the assembled faithful's greeting of welcome to the Lord **who is about to speak to them** and as an expression of their faith through song.

The Alleluia or the verse before the gospel must be sung and during it all stand. It is not to be sung only by the cantor who intoned it or by the choir, but by the whole congregation together. [23]

This paragraph from the *GIL* is not a familiar text in parishes where the *Alleluia!* is recited. Speaking it is like reciting 'Happy Birthday' – the *Alleluia!* is a shout of joy and only makes sense when sung. It is not difficult to find two or three *Alleluias* which can be sung unaccompanied if necessary so that singing becomes the norm.

• The Homily

sets forth the mysteries of faith and the standards of the Christian life on the basis of the sacred text. It should be regarded as an integral part of the Liturgy of the Word. Preaching is one of the priest's or deacon's most important tasks, and during the homily the reader like the rest of the assembly becomes a Listener (see p.12).

• Silence

The liturgy of the word must be celebrated in a way that fosters meditation; clearly, any sort of haste that hinders reflectiveness must be avoided. **The dialogue between God and his people** taking place through the Holy Spirit **demands short intervals of silence**, suited to the assembly, as an opportunity to take the word of God to heart and to prepare a response to it in prayer.

Proper times for silence during the liturgy of the word are...before this liturgy begins, **after the first and the second reading, after the homily**. [28]

• The Profession of Faith

Its purpose here is to give the gathered faithful the opportunity to respond and give assent to the word of God heard in the readings and through the homily. [29]

• General Intercessions or the Prayer of the Faithful

After listening to the liturgy of the word and responding to it, the faithful pray for the needs of the universal Church and the local community, for the salvation of the world and those oppressed by any burden, and for special categories of people. [30]

The treatment of the General Intercessions in most parishes suggests that more attention needs to be given to both preparing and delivering them. Everything that will be said later about public speech will apply to the General Intercessions as well.

2d. What aids are there to the proper celebration of the Liturgy of the Word?

• A place for proclaiming the word of God –

There must be a place in the church that is somewhat elevated, fixed, and of a suitable design and nobility. [32]

Because the lectern (ambo) is the place from which ministers proclaim the word of God, it must of its nature be reserved for the readings, the responsorial psalm, and the Easter proclamation (Exsultet). It may rightly be used for the homily and the general intercessions because of their close connection with the entire liturgy of the word. It is better for the commentator, cantor, director of singing, for example, not to use the lectern. [33]

• Books for proclaiming the word of God

...the books containing the readings of the word of God remind the hearers of the presence of God speaking to his people. Since...the books too serve as signs and symbols of the sacred, care must be taken to ensure that they truly are worthy and beautiful. [35]

Because of the dignity of the word of God, the books of readings used in the celebration are not to be replaced by other pastoral aids, for example, by leaflets printed for the faithful's preparation of the readings or for their personal meditation. [37]

2e. What offices and ministries are involved in the Liturgy of the Word and what are their roles?

• The Presider

The one presiding at the liturgy of the word brings the spiritual nourishment to those present, especially in the homily. Even if he too is a listener to the word of God proclaimed by others, the duty of proclaiming it has been entrusted above all to him. Personally or through others he sees to it that the word of God is properly proclaimed. He then as a rule reserves to himself the task of composing comments to help the people to listen more attentively and to preach a homily that fosters in them a richer understanding of the word of God. [38]

• The Faithful

i. …the congregation of the faithful still today receives from God the word of his covenant through the faith that comes **by hearing**. [45]

ii. For their part, the faithful at the celebration of Mass **are to listen to the word of God** with an inward and outward reverence that will bring them continuous growth in the spiritual life and draw them more deeply into the mystery they celebrate." [45]

iii. [Love of the scriptures] is…the force that renews the entire people of God. All the faithful **without exception** must therefore always be ready to **listen gladly** to God's word. When this word is proclaimed in the Church and put into living practice, it enlightens the faithful through the working of the Holy Spirit and draws them into the entire mystery of the Lord as a reality to be lived. [48]

iv. **When they hear the word of God** and reflect deeply on it, the faithful receive the power to respond to it actively with full faith, hope, and charity through prayer and self-giving, and not only during Mass but in their entire Christian life. [48]

Emphasis has been put on the role of the faithful during the Liturgy of the Word to make clear that the action expected of them here is **listening**. Unfortunately in many churches there is a mistaken belief that people should be reading along with the reader. This is especially true in places where Missalettes are used. But reading and listening are not the same thing: in fact, reading is generally an obstacle to listening and gets in the way of hearing properly.

This habit has arisen partly because this is what many think Missalettes are for. But resort to them may be a refuge from poor proclamation of the Word by readers. Whatever the case, it would be counterproductive to make a frontal assault on them. The most effective means of getting the assembly to put them down is to ensure that the readings are well proclaimed so that people come to see they are not neeeded. The parish should also make sure that there is a good sound system suited to the space and adequate for people who have difficulty hearing.

The Deacon

proclaims the gospel, sometimes gives the homily, and proposes the intentions of the general intercessions to the people.

The Reader

1. The reader has his own proper function in the eucharistic celebration and should exercise this even though ministers of a higher rank may be present. [51; quoted from *GIRM* 66]

2. The liturgical assembly truly requires readers…. Proper measures must therefore be taken to ensure that there are **qualified lay persons who have been trained to carry out this ministry**. Whenever there is more than one reading, it is better to assign the readings to different readers, if available. [52]

3. **It is necessary that those who exercise the ministry of reader… be truly qualified and carefully prepared so that the faithful may develop a warm and living love for Scripture from listening to the sacred texts read.** [Quoted from *GIRM* 66]

   Their preparation must above all be spiritual, but what may be called a technical preparation is also needed. The spiritual preparation presupposes at least a biblical and liturgical formation. The purpose of their biblical formation is to give readers the ability to understand the readings in context and to equip the readers to have some grasp of the meaning and structure of the liturgy of the word and of the significance of its connection with the liturgy of the eucharist. The technical preparation should make the readers more skilled in the art of reading publicly, either with power of their own voice or with the help of sound equipment. [55]

The psalmist (the cantor/singer of the psalm)

is responsible for singing, responsorially or directly, the chants between the readings – the psalm or other biblical canticle,…the Alleluia or other chant. [56]

The commentator

This genuine liturgical ministry

> .. consists in presenting to the assembly of the faithful, from a suitable place, relevant explanations and comments that are clear, of marked simplicity, meticulously prepared, as a rule written out, and approved beforehand by the celebrant. [57]

This ministry was of most value in the years immediately following the introduction of the changes to the Mass after Vatican II. As we have become accustomed to the rites in the vernacular the need for a commentator has all but disappeared.

B. THE BIBLE

1. Getting acquainted with the Bible

Although we have been fed with a much richer selection of readings from the Bible since the revision of the Lectionary, many Catholics are still not at ease with our Book. Many older Catholics were brought up to think that the Bible belonged to Protestants, that it was not a book to be read by ordinary people but a place to record important family dates: births, marriages and deaths. At first sight, the Old Testament especially seems remote from our times and concerns with its unpronounceable names, unfamiliar images, and incredible stories. This attitude is changing as the appetite for Bible study grows. But it is essential that those who proclaim Scripture at Mass work to understand and love the Bible so that they help those who listen to understand that it is the story of our life. 'Every Bible story is a metaphor for the many experiences of God we have all had and will have in our lives.'[2]

It is very likely that most Catholics own a Bible, but in conducting readers' courses, I have found the summary in the personal study edition of the New American Bible to be very useful and have rearranged the information on the Old Testament for convenience as follows:[3]

2. The Books of the Old Testament

Introductory Note

The word 'Bible' comes from Greek, where it is actually a plural word, 'the books'. This helps us understand that the Bible is not a single book, but a number of books collected together in two large groupings, the Old and New Testaments. 'Testament' translates the Hebrew word which means 'covenant' – promise.

So the Bible is a collection of books which tells us about the covenant or promise God made with Israel through Moses (the old or first covenant) which he fulfilled in Jesus (the new or second covenant).

The Old Testament is common to both Jews and Christians, with some differences. Jews, followed by Protestants, recognise only the books written in Hebrew, of which there are 39. Catholics recognise in addition seven other books written in Greek which we call deutero-canonical – books which were added to the 'canon' (the official list, the rule of faith) at a secondary stage. These books are: Tobit, Judith, 1 and 2 Maccabees, Wisdom, Ecclesiasticus (or Sirach), and Baruch. Judaism reverences them and considers them sacred, but they are not part of their canon. Protestants call these books The Apocrypha. Also in this catagory are some passages in the books of Daniel and Esther (indicated !!) which were written in Greek.

In the list which follows, the abbreviations for books of the Bible are those used by the New Jerusalem Bible, and the deutero-canonical books included in the Catholic Bible but omitted by Protestants are printed in italics.

The New Testament is identical for all Christians and consists of 27 books.

a. The Pentateuch

Genesis (Gn)
Exodus (Ex)
Leviticus (Lv)
Numbers (Nb)
Deuteronomy (Dt)

The name *Pentateuch* means a 5-part writing – one book in five volumes. They are called *Torah* in Jewish tradition, and contain the basic teachings of the Jewish faith. Tradition assigns authorship to Moses, but scholars agree they were written by several authors and acquired their present form over the course of centuries.

b. The Historical Books

Joshua (Jos)
Judges (Jg)
Ruth (Rt)
I Samuel (1 S)
II Samuel (2 S)
I Kings (1 K)
II Kings (2 K)

These seven books can be called the *Deuteronomistic History* because the Book of Deuteronomy serves as a kind of preface to the whole collection. The writers of these books have taken many stories and combined them to explain why the nation collapsed and why the people were led into exile. They wanted to express a simple message to their audience: learn from the past.

Later Histories

I Chronicles (1 Ch)
II Chronicles (2 Ch)
Ezra (Ezr)
Nehemiah (Ne)
Tobit (To)
Judith (Jdt)
Esther (Est) **!!**
I Maccabees (1 M)
II Maccabees (2 M)

Scholars identify the Chroniclers' history as one of the three major units telling the story of the Israelite people. Like the Deuteronomistic History outlined above, this group of books tells the story of the Israelite kingdoms and their fall. But while the deuteronomic history tries to explain why they fell, the chroniclers' real purpose is to outline the prospects for Israel's future.

c. The Wisdom Books

Job (Jb)

A dramatic poem that treats the problem of suffering of the innocent and retribution

Psalms (Ps)

A collection of religious songs under the major headings of hymns,laments, and songs of thanksgiving

Proverbs (Pr)

An anthology of mostly short sayings in poetical form whose purpose is to teach wisdom for successful living

Ecclesiastes/
Qoheleth (Qo)

A treatise on the emptiness of all things, concerned with the purpose and value of human life

Song of Songs (Sg)

A collection of love poems full of sensuous imagery which can be seen as a portrayal of ideal human love

Wisdom (Ws)

Written in the Jewish community of Alexandria about 100 years before Christ. It explains traditions and themes familiar to Judaism but reinterprets them from the experience of living in a Hellenistic (Greek) culture

Ecclesiasticus/
Sirach (Si)

A collection of proverbs containing moral instruction, written to show that real wisdom wasto be found in the traditions of Israel and not in the godless philosophy of the day

◼ d. The Prophets

The major prophets:

Isaiah (Is)

Jeremiah (Jr)

Lamentations (Lm)

Baruch (Ba)

Ezekiel (Ezk)

Daniel (Dn) !!

Though written later than the period to which they refer, these books follow a similar pattern. The prophet experiences life within a believing community which nourishes his relationship with God. Sometime during the prophet's life, God is experienced more profoundly; he develops an acute sensitivity to violations of justice, especially to the poor and rejected, and feels compelled to call these incidents to the attention of the community with warnings of the consequences. He reminds them that God's love and peace will be manifest if the people look after the poor and work for justice.

The minor prophets

Hosea (Ho)

Joel (Jl)

Amos (Am)

Obadiah (Ob)

Jonah (Jon)

Micah (Mi)

Nahum (Na)

Habakkuk (Hab)

Zephaniah (Zp)

Haggai (Hg)

Zechariah (Zc)

Malachi (Ml)

These prophets are called minor because their writings are short compared to the major prophets. Each author wrote to deal with a specific situation of his own time, but a common pattern is nevertheless observable: sin followed by judgment followed by salvation or the promise of restoration. Taken together, these books are both a reflection on the past and a lesson for the future. Those editing them were greatly influenced by the theology of Deuteronomy – sin does not go unpunished, but God is merciful and wants only the repentance and restoration of Israel. The call to repentance is heard throughout this collection.

Types of writing in the Old Testament

While writers use various terms to describe the kinds of writing in the Old Testament, many of them quite different from what we are accustomed to today, the basic divisions are:
- **narrative** (stories and epics),
- **poetry** (many of the prophets, and especially the psalms)
- **discourse** or **argument** (teachings, explanations or solemn pronouncements), and
- **everything else**.

Each type of writing requires a different kind of proclamation. For instance, the creation stories are not meant to be read as fact: Charpentier accurately describes them as 'a liturgical poem'.[4] Preparation begins with identifying the type of reading.

Exercise 1

Read the following passages and decide:
   a) which type of writing each piece is (list on previous page)
   b) what special problems the reading might pose
   c) which of the readings you are most comfortable with

a.

God put Abraham to the test. 'Abraham, Abraham,' he called. 'Here I am', he replied. 'Take your son,' God said 'your only child Isaac, whom you love, and go to the land of Moriah. There you shall offer him as a burnt offering, on a mountain I will point out to you.

Rising early next morning Abraham saddled his ass and took with him two of his servants and his son Isaac. He chopped wood for the burnt offering and started on his journey to the place God had pointed out to him. On the third day Abraham looked up and saw the place in the distance. Then Abraham said to his servants, 'Stay here with the donkey. The boy and I will go over there; we will worship and come back to you.'

Abraham took the wood for the burnt offering, loaded it on Isaac, and carried in his own hands the fire and the knife. Then the two of them set out together. Isaac spoke to his father Abraham, 'Father' he said. 'Yes, my son' he replied. 'Look,' he said 'here are the fire and the wood, but where is the lamb for the burnt offering?' Abraham answered, 'My son, God himself will provide the lamb for the burnt offering.' Then the two of them went on together.

When they arrived at the place God had pointed out to him, Abraham built an altar there and arranged the wood. Then he bound his son Isaac and put him on the altar on top of the wood. Abraham stretched out his hand andseized the knife to kill his son.

But the angel of the Lord called to him from heaven, 'Abraham, Abraham' he said. 'I am here' he replied. 'Do not raise your hand against the boy' the angel said. 'Do not harm him, for now I know you fear God. You have not refused me your son, your only son.' Then looking up, Abraham saw a ram caught by its horns in a bush. Abraham took the ram and offered it as a burnt offering in place of his son. Abraham called this place 'The Lord provides', and hence the saying today: On the mountain the Lord provides.

The angel of the Lord called Abraham a second time from heaven. 'I swear by my own self – it is the Lord who speaks – because you have done this, because you have not refused me your son, your only son, I will shower blessings on you, I will make your descendants as many as the stars of heaven and the grains of sand on the seashore. Your descendants shall gain possession of the gates of their enemies. All the nations of the earth shall bless themselves by your descendants as a reward for your obedience.'

Genesis 22: 1-18, prescribed as the 2nd Reading for the Easter Vigil

b.   Thus says the Lord:

Now your creator will be your husband,
his name, the Lord of hosts;
your redeemer will be the Holy One of Israel,
he is called the God of the whole earth.
Yes, like a forsaken wife, distressed in spirit,
the Lord calls your back.
Does a man cast off the wife of his youth?
asks your God.

I did forsake you for a brief moment,
but with great love will I take you back.
In excess of anger, for a moment
I hid my face from you.
But with everlasting love I have taken pity on you,
says the Lord, your redeemer.

I am now as I was in the days of Noah
when I swore that Noah's waters
should never flood the world again.
So now I swear concerning my anger with you
and the threats I made against you;

for the mountains may depart,
the hills be shaken,
but my love for you will never leave you
and my covenant of peace with you will never be shaken,
says the Lord who takes pity on you.

Unhappy creature, storm-tossed, disconsolate,
see, I will set your stones on carbuncles
and your foundations on sapphires.
I will make rubies your battlements,
your gates crystal,
and your entire wall precious stones.
Your sons will all be taught by the Lord.
The prosperity of your sons will be great.
You will be founded on integrity;
remote from oppression, you will have nothing to fear,
remote from terror, it will not approach you.

Isaiah 54: 5-14, prescribed as the 4th Reading for the Easter Vigil

c. Moses spoke to the people and said:

'So now, O Israel,
what does the Lord your God require of you?
Only to fear the Lord your God,
to walk in all his ways, to love him,
to serve the Lord your God
with all your heart and with all your soul,
and to keep the commandments of the Lord your God
and his decrees that I am commanding you today,
for your own well-being.

'You shall put these words of mine in your heart and soul,
and you shall bind them as a sign of your hand,
and fix them as an emblem on your forehead,
teach them to your children, talking about them
when you are at home and when you are away,
when you lie down and when you rise.

'Write them on the doorposts of your house and on your gates,
so that your days and the days of your children
may be multiplied in the land
that the Lord swore to your ancestors to give them,
as long as the heavens are above the earth.

'If you will diligently observe this entire commandment
that I am commanding you,
loving the Lord your God, walking in all his ways,
and holding fast to him,
then the Lord will drive out all these nations before you,
and you will dispossess nations larger and mightier than yourselves.
Every place on which you set foot shall be yours;
your territory shall extend
from the wilderness to the Lebanon and from the River,
the river Euphrates, to the Western Sea.
No one will be able to stand against you;
the Lord your God will put the fear and dread of you
on all the land on which you set foot, as he promised you.

'See, I am setting before you today a blessing and a curse:
the blessing,
if you obey the commandments of the Lord your God
that I am commanding you today;
and the curse,
if you do not obey the commandments of the Lord your God,
but turn from the way that I am commanding you today,
to follow other gods that you have not known.

Deuteronomy 10: 12-13. 11: 18-28

3. The Books of the New Testament

• The Gospels

are the narrations attributed to Matthew, Mark, Luke and John, which contain the stories of the life, teaching, miracles, passion, death and resurrection of Jesus. Not biographies or histories, they are proclamations of the great work God has done for us through his Son, the 'Good News' (the meaning of the word Gospel).

The writings attributed to Matthew, Mark and Luke (their names are not mentioned in the text) are called the 'synoptic' Gospels, from the Greek word meaning 'at a glance'. This refers to the fact that the three accounts are similar, covering more or less the same events and words of Jesus, which helps establish that they used many of the same sources.

Mark's gospel was the first to be written, Matthew incorporates much of it in his narration, together with material from another source. Luke in turn made use of the accounts of both Mark and Matthew, plus an additional source of his own.

John's Gospel is a rather different kind of book, with elements of poetry and reflection, starting with its famous Prologue, read on Christmas Day. It describes fewer events in the ministry of Jesus than the Synoptics, but at greater length.

• The Acts of the Apostles

also attributed to Luke, continues the story of the early followers of Jesus after his ascent into heaven and contains the development of the early church and its spread to other peoples and places.

• The Letters (Epistles)

are of two types. Most of them were written by Paul to communities he had founded (with the exception of the Letter to the Romans). They were designed to instruct, scold, encourage, correct and update the various churches. Although scholars do not think he wrote all the letters attributed to him, those bearing his name are Romans, 1 and 2 Corinthians, Galatians, Ephesians, Philippians, Colossians, 1 and 2 Thessalonians, 1 and 2 Timothy, Titus and Philemon. The Letter to the Hebrews is an anonymous work. The other letters are styled *Letters to all Christians* because they were not addressed to a specific community. These are James, 1 and 2 Peter, 1, 2, 3 John, and Jude, but the names do not necessarily imply authorship.

• The Book of Revelation

is a book of prophecy by an author who calls himself John (not the same John to whom the fourth Gospel is attributed). It is an example of a special type of writing called 'apocalyptic' which would have been understood by the churches of Asia Minor in the 1st century. It can present difficulties to modern readers, arising from the problem of understanding the purpose of this type of writing, and the historical and cultural situation it comes from. There is a tendency in certain quarters to take it literally (this is what fundamentalism means) though this is to misunderstand it.

C. FROM BIBLE TO LECTIONARY

The scriptures that we listen to during liturgy are contained in a book called a Lectionary, which means a selection taken from a larger work, in this case, the Bible. The readings we hear are not random extracts, but the result of careful choice on the part of a special commission set up after Vatican II to fulfill the design expressed by the *Constitution on the Sacred Liturgy*:

> The treasures of the Bible are to be opened up more lavishly, so that a richer share in God's word may be provided for the faithful. In this way a more representative portion of holy Scripture will be read to the people in the course *of the prescribed number of years.'* [51]

Among the principles that guided the development of the lectionary were: that the entire Old Testament is presupposed in Christ's teaching, his actions and his suffering; that there are other important themes in scripture beside the central one of Christ's suffering, death and resurrection; and that the liturgical year provides the ideal means of presenting the message of salvation to the faithful in an organised way.[6]

The first lectionary of 1969 provided for three readings at the Sunday eucharist: one from the Hebrew Bible, one non-gospel reading from the New Testament, and one gospel reading, beside a Responsorial Psalm. The one-year cycle of readings in use before Vatican II was replaced by a three-year cycle for Sundays (with three readings) and a two-year cycle for weekdays (with two readings).

A new edition in 1981 made some minor changes, but more importantly included a greatly expanded Introduction which is found at the front of Volume I of the Lectionary. This *General Introduction to the Lectionary* is the basis for understanding the Ministry of the Word and all Readers are advised to read it through completely and return to it often. This Workbook is based on the guidelines it contains.

The *General Introduction* defines clearly the way in which the readings are arranged for Sundays and Solemnities:

> The principles governing the Order of Readings for Sundays and the solemnities of the Lord are called the principles of 'harmony' and of 'semicontinuous reading'. One or the other applies according to the different seasons of the year and the distinctive character of the particular liturgical season. [66.3]

> The best instance of harmony between the Old and New Testament

readings occurs when it is one that Scripture itself suggests. This is the case when the teaching and events recounted in texts of the New Testament bear a more or less explicit relationship to the teaching and events of the Old Testament. The present Order of Readings selects Old Testament texts mainly because of their correlation with New Testament texts read in the same Mass, and particularly with the gospel text.

Harmony of another kind exists between texts of the readings for each Mass during Advent, Lent, Easter, the seasons that have a distinctive importance or character.

In contrast, the Sundays in Ordinary Time do not have a distinctive character. Thus the texts of both the apostolic and gospel readings are arranged in an order of semi-continuous reading, whereas the Old Testament reading is harmonised with the gospel. [67]

The complete list of readings for the Sundays of all three liturgical years and the major feasts is given in Appendix A (page 46).

PART TWO

Improving Proclamation

Contents of Part Two: A: Reflection; B: Research (p.24); C:Rehearsal (p.26); D: Review (p.21); E: Special Situations (p.30)

A. Reflection

1. Begin preparation early – 10 days/two weeks
2. Listening and telling:
   Work with one or more partners to bring the readings to life.
3. Read the passage aloud many times.
4. Pray with the text: find its meaning for you.

There are two aspects to being a reader which might be called internal and external. The external aspect is everything to do with the public proclamation of the assigned passage, reading the text aloud in church to the assembly. This will be considered later under the heading **Rehearsal**. Before public proclamation happens and as preparation for the external aspect, there is the internal preparation that the reader makes: reflection on the text. This section addresses the reader's need for spiritual preparation as called for in the *GIL*:

> Their preparation must above all be spiritual, but what may be called a technical preparation is also needed. The spiritual preparation presupposes at least a biblical and liturgical formation. The purpose of their biblical formation is to give readers the ability to understand the readings in context and to equip the readers to have some grasp of the meaning and structure of the liturgy of the word and of the significance of its connection with the liturgy of the eucharist. [55]

1. Starting two weeks before the date

scheduled for the reading may seems an impossible counsel of perfection. But, if the passage is to be well proclaimed, the reader needs an understanding of the text as well as practise in delivering it aloud. All of this takes time, especially at the beginning or when the individual reader is refreshing his/her preparation skills.

2. Listening and telling

is a technique based on the desirability of sharing insights with others. Readers take it in turn to read the passage in question and then share briefly the word, image, idea, question that it suggests to them. After each member of the small group (three is a good number) has read the passage, individuals are invited to share with the others what meaning the passage has for them personally. This is a form of *lectio divina* in which the focus is on a word or passage from the text which has particular resonance for the individual. This is a valuable form of faith-sharing. In addition, the one who will proclaim the passage benefits from the insights of others and gains a deeper understanding than would be possible working alone.

3. Reading the passage aloud

is important because it accustoms the reader to the sound of the passage and is quite different from reading silently to oneself. This is a form of rehearsal and will enable the reader to take into account the technical points to be made later. But it is part of reflection as well and appears here first.

4. The context in which all preparation of sacred scripture takes place

is prayer. The reader should aim to make the text personal prayer, to use it as prayer. By doing this and following the other steps suggested here, the reader will come to an understanding of the meaning of the passage. The power of the public proclamation arises from the reader's understanding of the passage. The purpose of **Reflection** as the first step is to help the reader acquire this understanding.

B. Research

5. Check correct pronunciation of place and proper names.
6. Read the passage in its proper context in the scriptures –
    read what comes before and after it and what might have been left out.
7. Study scripture commentaries.
8. Find answers to questions raised by the text –
    1) What was the author's reason for writing?
    2) What is the literary style?
    3) What is the mood? Does it change in the course of the piece?
    4) How would the original community have heard the passage?
    5) How will our community hear this message?

This section deals with questions raised by the text. Finding answers to them and any others which come out of the preparation enable the reader to feel comfortable with the passage and develop a better understanding of it.

5. Correct pronunciation is important

Most readers will have had the awful experience of being tripped up by a word during their reading. Most readers will also be aware that this is the result of not having prepared well enough. The first look at the passage will reveal likely pitfalls which can be removed by checking on correct pronunciation. If the parish doesn't have a pronunciation guide, this might be a excellent purchase for the peace of mind of the congregation as well as the readers!

◼ 6. Reading the passage in context

This is a reminder that the lectionary is not the Bible and that the meaning of the passages for any given Sunday may not be clear as they stand. The readings need to be seen in their proper setting with what precedes them, what follows them, and what has been omitted. The people who selected the readings, especially the first reading, had the intention of preparing the assembly to listen to the gospel. But the text may not be clear without checking.

A good example is the 13th Sunday in Ordinary Time, Year A, when the First Reading is taken from the second book of the Kings 4: 8-11. 14-16, which means chapter 4, verses 8 to 11, and verses 14 to 16. Remembering that the first reading has been selected to harmonise with the Gospel, the reader needs to look at the passage from Matthew (10: 37-42) to understand the way in which the text from Kings fits with it: 'Anyone who welcomes a prophet because he is a prophet, will have a prophet's reward; and anyone who welcomes a holy man because he is a holy man will have a holy man's reward'. This is a truly wonderful message – that the generosity of God far exceeds anything we could expect.

But there is more to the story of the Shunemite women than this and, in order to understand the context of this passage, the reader will need to look at what comes before verse 8 in chapter 4, and perhaps what the previous chapters are about. Verses 12 and 13 are not included in the passage but need to be looked at, and the verses which follow verse 16 as well. The missing material may not always be relevant, but it is important that you check to make sure. In this case, to neglect this step is to miss the opportunity to learn a much richer story and to meet one of the best-drawn female characters of the Old Testament.

Once the context of an individual passage has been established, the reader then needs to get an overall view of all the texts for the Sunday: the key passage is the Gospel (see pp 21-22 above). In the major liturgical seasons, the first and second readings will have been chosen to harmonise with it, while in Ordinary Time this will be true only of the first reading. In all seasons, the Psalm and especially the antiphon will help the reader understand the focus of all the passages.

◼ 7. Study the scripture commentaries

This recommendation may seem to come later in the process than expected; some people may be tempted to go immediately to an authoritative source to find out 'what the passage means'. But this would short-circuit an important aspect of the preparation – work to discover a personal connection.

The place to begin is with an understanding of what the passage means to the individual reader gained through reflection and prayer alone and with others. Once this has happened, the commentaries of scholars and others will be helpful in suggesting further aspects – including historical, cultural, social – which might not have occurred to the reader. Commentaries can be very helpful and the reader's preparation is not complete without making use of them. But which ones should be used? In Appendix C (p.59) are extracts from a range of sources which might help you descide what could be recommended for the parish. On p.70 there is a more complete Reading List.

■ 8. Find answers to questions raised by the text.

The best commentaries and a study edition of the Bible will deal very well with the first four points. Examples can be found in Appendix C. The response to the final question – 'How will our community hear this message?' – begins with the reflection and prayer of the reader in preparing the text, joined to an understanding of the members of the parish and the larger community around it.

C. Rehearsal

9. Make use of basic communication skills:
  – Body language
  – Speed and volume of delivery
  – Eye contact
10. Practise with the microphone you will use in church.
11. Get help: ask a friend to listen critically.
12. Tape/video yourself reading.

■ 9. The reader needs to develop basic communication skills

so that the proclamations benefit from good delivery. The value of this is recognised in the *General Introduction to the Lectionary*:

> Their preparation must above all be spiritual, but what may be called a technical preparation is also needed…. The technical preparation should make the readers more skilled in the art of reading publicly, either with power of their own voice or with the help of sound equipment. [55]

i) Body language

gives information to the assembly before the reader has said a word. The reader's walk from a place in the assembly to the ambo, the posture before the book, the position of the hands and feet – all of these tell the community about the reader's attitude and whether they are confident and prepared for what they are about to do.

The reader's aim should be a relaxed purposefulness which allows everyone to concentrate on the spoken word with no distraction. The only way to achieve this is through practice. After a certain amount of experience, the reader will know in his body when movement – to and from the ambo and posture while there – serves to enhance the proclamation.

ii)   Speed and volume of delivery

indicate to the assembly how much preparation the reader has done. Most readers go too fast; this is usually because their preparation has been inadequate – the passage is 'undercooked'. Again, the remedy is practice in the place where the proclamation will be delivered. It will help if the reader listens carefully as he/she reads, remembering that the assembly cannot listen as fast as a reader can read. Delivery that is too fast is partly responsible for the assembly's unfortunate practice of reading along instead of listening. The reader must deliver the reading at a pace which helps clarify the meaning, and with enough volume for all to hear without difficulty. Neglect of these two aspects will undermine all the good work done in preparing the text.

Communication depends on the voice: much can be done during preparation by paying attention to such things as good articulation, word colour, the occurrence of action words, the use of pauses, phrasing and emphasis. There are exercises in the appendix to help with this.

iii)   Eye contact

If it is remembered that the reading of scripture in liturgy is a form of communication, then the need for eye contact is clear. The message is being delivered by the one proclaiming to the assembly who are listening: part of the communication is eye contact. Normally we would not consider speaking to someone without looking them in the eye, especially if the message is important. When we come to scripture during the Sunday Mass, what could be more important? Making eye contact is one of the ways the reader conveys to the gathering that there is a connection between them and the passage: that the message is meant for them.

Two places should be considered separately for eye contact: the introduction to the reading – 'A reading from the prophet Isaiah'[7] – and the closing – 'The word of the Lord'. But the reader needs to decide where eye contact will be made in the *body* of the text. Usually there are only three or four such places. The reader should know the text well enough to look up during the few words previously selected and actually make eye contact. Avoid the searchlight technique where the eyes scan from left to right without settling, or speaking to the angels by addressing the ceiling at the back of the church. Practise with other readers scattered in church, asking them after your reading to say whether you made eye contact with them. The whole process may feel uncomfortable at first, but when done well, it will contribute to a more powerful proclamation and help the assembly feel connected to the message.

Here are some phrases for practice in making eye contact:[8]

> I tell you, brothers and sisters, the time is short.
>
> The grace of God has appeared, offering salvation to all.
>
> Are you not aware that we who were baptized into Christ Jesus were baptized into his death?
>
> If God is for us, who can be against us?

10. Microphone technique

is essential if all the good work of preparation is not to be wasted. Because every microphone and sound system is different, it is really important for every reader to find out what is the best position for them. This is best done with the help of others so that adjustments can be made. Unfortunately, some sound systems in churches are inadequate or inappropriate; their replacement might be moved up the list of priorities for the parish budget since being able to hear the word of God is so important. In the meantime, the reader's preparation should include doing whatever is necessary to make it easy for the assembly to hear clearly what God is saying to them.

Ray Longergan offers the following exercise to improve use with the microphone:[9]

> And powdery brown-backed bumblebees busily buzz by.
>
> Frail poppies, white and faintly pink.
>
> With beaded bubbles winking at the brim.
>
> Speak the speech, I pray you as I pronounce it to you,
> trippingly on the tongue.
>
> Peter Piper, the pepper picker, picked a peck of pickled peppers. A peck of pickled peppers did Peter Piper, the pepper picker, pick. If Peter Piper, the pepper picker, picked a peck of pickled peppers, where is the peck of pickled peppers that Peter Piper, the pepper picker, picked?

11. Get a friend to listen critically

before the Sunday of your reading. The need for rehearsal is more pressing for those new to this ministry. It consists of asking someone to give reliable feedback on all the matters that have been part of the reader's preparation: the technical aspects – speed of delivery, adequate volume, and eye contact – but overall, whether the delivery is convincing. Does the reader believe the message contained in the passage?

D. Review

12. Evaluate your interpretations and delivery.

13. Get a trusted friend to provide a critique.

12. When the reading is over

The general tendency is to feel that the reader's work is done once the reading is over. Relief at having got through it is a natural feeling. But there is great benefit to be gained by taking the time to reflect on the reading a few days after it: in order to see what went well and what could be improved, as well as why it could. The question to ask is: How well did I do what I intended? Many readers have had the experience of suddenly seeing something new as they are proclaiming the passage they prepared. This new insight is valuable and should be examined more carefully after the liturgy is over. It is only by reflecting in this way that the reader can learn useful lessons and make improvements for next time.

13. A friend listening

This is a book-end to item 11: it helps to have a friend to listen to the reading before it is given and to give feedback after the proclamation. The items to be covered are the same: the technical aspects and whether the proclamation was convincing.

Further thoughts:

One reader per reading

The general practice should be for there to be one reader for each reading.
The reason for this is clear, given the amount of preparation recommended. Equally compelling is the fact that the Old Testament reading is separated by centuries from the readings of the New Testament: one clear way to convey this is to use different voices to proclaim them. The *General Introduction to the Lectionary* makes this recommendation:

> Whenever there is more than one reading, it is better to assign the readings to different readers, if possible. [52]

The importance of silence

The *GIL* emphasises the importance of silence in article 28 (see page 10 above) and points out that any form of haste hinders the reflectiveness desired.

How should this silence be incorporated into the liturgy of the word? The three places where it should happen are after the first and second reading, and after the homily. The length of the silence can be in the keeping of the first and second reader. There are two ways of doing it: after the text of the reading and before the closing phrase 'The word of the Lord', the reader can stand at the ambo with bowed head for the desired length of time before raising his/her head, looking at the assembly and saying the closing phrase. Or the silence can be introduced after the closing phrase with the reader remaining at the ambo for the period of silence, signalling its end by leaving the ambo. The first option seems more satisfactory because the silence is incorporated in a way that makes it part of the reader's proclamation.

Not too long between reading duties

Readers should aim to make their proclamation better each successive time. For this to happen, the reader needs to be scheduled at reasonably close intervals. In some places, readers find they are needed only four times a year: this is too great an interval to build up experience and means that each time the reader has to start from scratch.

There are two remedies for this situation.

The first is to ensure that each reading is assigned to a separate reader. This will mean there are at least two names on the list for each Sunday. In addition, the General Intercessions might be assigned to a third reader.

Secondly, it might be advisable to recommission readers after a period of study and re-skilling. After parish readers as a group have been through a period of study, they should be publicly commissioned for a fixed term, say, two or three years, after which they can be recommissioned if they are needed, or retired for a period while new readers take their place.

This point is a reminder that readers will benefit from regular meetings for prayer and discussion of the scripture for each season. It helps readers of particular texts to see how the passage assigned to them fits into the overall pattern and work toward a more coherent presentation of the whole season.

E. Special Situations

1. The Psalm, especially when not sung

2. Preparing readings from Paul's letters

3. The Book of Revelation

1. The Psalm, especially when not sung

We usually assume there are three readings from Scripture at the Sunday Mass: the first and second reading, and the Gospel. There are, in fact, four – the Psalm is also the Word of God and deserves equal attention.

It was the practice in the Jewish synagogue, which continues to the present day, to use the word of God contained in the Psalm as a response to the word of God proclaimed in the first reading. It is used for its own sake, does not accompany any other action during the liturgy, and may not be replaced by a non-scriptural text.

What is the reason for this importance? One author says:

The 150 psalms express Israel's experience of the Holy One, directly and concretely, with a wide range of feeling.[10]

Compiled by a succession of psalmists over centuries, marked by the ancient Near Eastern tradition of hymnody, they express the full range of human experience and emotion so well that they work for us today as well as they did when first composed. They have never been added to, because there has been no need: whatever we want to express to God – of thanksgiving, of praise, of petition, lament or anger – has already been given voice in vivid poetry which links us to our ancestors in faith. Another author says:

The psalms lead us through the sections or rooms of our life, always ending with a strong Amen. Walking along, we are never alone but in the company of our saintly ancestors. When our questions arise, as happened to the two persons on their way to Emmaus, Jesus appears to declare that 'everything written about me in the law of Moses and in the prophets and *psalms* must be fulfilled' (Luke 24: 44). Through the psalms Jesus opens our minds to the hidden mysteries within our lives.[11]

Against this background, how should the psalms be treated at Sunday Mass?

We begin with the fact that the word itself – psalm – comes from the stringed instrument used to accompany the sung poetry. The *General Introduction to the Lectionary* makes clear the expectation that the Psalm will be sung

> As a rule, the responsorial psalm should be sung. [20]

The document then goes on to offer encouragement to the congregation to sing: by giving alternative texts for the response which don't change each Sunday. It is also possible to use seasonal psalms [89], that is, the same psalm is sung for a number of Sundays with the advantage that the community comes to know the psalm well and is better able to make the prayer theirs.

Reciting the psalm

However, if it is not possible to sing it, the *General Introduction* says that the psalm

> is to be recited in a manner conducive to meditation on the word of God. [22]

How is this to be done?

First of all, the reader needs to recognise that the psalm is poetry which means that imagery and rhythm are important. In the Acknowledgements section of the Lectionary which contains the readings for Sundays and Solemnities is the information that the version of the Psalms used is provided by the Grail. 'These translations directly from the Hebrew rather than the earlier Latin translation from Greek, were made possible by the progress in biblical studies. They allowed the translator 'to stay close to this unique literary form, with its repetition of words, its own particular images, its stylistic peculiarities and its poetic rhythm.'[12] The expected difficulties of translating a poem are compounded in the case of the Psalms: 'When it is a matter of the word of God, where the historical nature of revelation has made content and form even more inseparable, the need for literary fidelity takes on special importance…'[13] For the reader, the most helpful result of using the Grail translation is that it make use of the rhythmic pattern of the original Hebrew.

If the psalm is not to be sung, the reader should start by being aware of the rhythmic pattern of the psalm prescribed. Examples are given below. In general, the unmarked version is so poetic that the rhythm suggests itself, but to make certain, the stress is given on the left for the first verse with the remainder left unmarked for the reader to complete.

■ a. Psalm 24

One of the seasonal psalms for Advent, used four times elsewhere in the lectionary.

1. Lord, make me know your ways,
   Lord, teach me your paths,
   Make me walk in your truth, and
        teach me:
   for you are God my saviour.

2. The Lord is good and upright.
   He shows the path to those who stray,
   he guides the humble in the right path;
   he teaches his way to the poor.

3. His ways are faithfulness and love
   for those who keep his covenant and will.
   The Lord's friendship is for those
        who revere him;
   to them he reveals his covenant.

1. Lórd, make me knów your wáys,
   Lórd, téach me your páths,
   Make me wálk in your trúth, and
        téach me:
   for yóu are Gód my sáviour.

2. The Lórd is góod and úpright.
   He shows the páth to thóse who stráy,
   he guides the húmble in the ríght páth;
   he téaches his wáy to the póor.

3. His wáys are fáithfulness and lóve
   for thóse who keep his cóvenant and wíll.
   The Lord's fríendship is for thóse
        who revére him;
   to thém he revéals his cóvenant.

■ b. Psalm 50

This is one of the seasonal psalms suggested for Lent and appears in the lectionary seven times, making use of different verses.

1. Have mercy on me, God, in your kindness.
   In your compassion blot out my offence.
   O wash me more and more from my guilt
   and cleanse me from my sin.

2. My offences truly I know them;
   my sin is always before me.
   Against you, you alone, have I sinned;
   what is evil in your sight I have done.

3. A pure heart create for me, O God,
   put a steadfast spirit within me.
   Do not cast me away from your presence,
   nor deprive me of your holy spirit.

4. Give me again the joy of your help;
   with a spirit of fervour sustain me.
   O Lord, open my lips
   and my mouth shall declare your praise.

1. Have mércy on me, Gód, in your kíndness.
   In your compássion blot óut my offénce.
   O wásh me more and móre from my guílt
   and cléanse me fróm my sín.

2. My offénces trúly I knów them;
   my sín is álways before me.
   Against yóu, you alóne, have I sínned;
   what is évil in your síght I have dóne.

3. A púre heart creáte for me, O Gód,
   put a stéadfast spírit withín me.
   Do not cást me awáy from your présence,
   nor deprive me of your hóly spírit.

4. Give me agáin the jóy of your hélp;
   with a spírit of férvour sustáin me.
   O Lórd, ópen my líps
   and my móuth shall decláre your práise.

The two psalms above are alike in having three beats per line. But there are other patterns such as those given opposite.

■ c. Psalm 26

1. The Lord is my light and my help;
   whom shall I fear?
   The Lord is the stronghold of my life;
   before whom shall I shrink?

2. There is one thing I ask of the Lord,
   for this I long,
   to live in the house of the Lord,
   all the days of my life,
   to savour the sweetness of the Lord,
   to behold his temple

3. I am sure I shall see the Lord's goodness
   in the land of the living.
   Hope in him, hold firm and take heart.
   Hope in the Lord!

The Lórd is my líght and my hélp;
whóm shall I féar?
The Lórd is the strónghold of my lífe;
before whóm shall I shrínk?

There is óne thing I ásk of the Lórd,
for thís I lóng,
to líve in the hóuse of the Lórd,
all the dáys of my lífe,
to sávour the swéetness of the Lórd,
to behóld his témple.

I am súre I shall sée the Lord's góodness
in the lánd of the líving.
Hope in hím, hold fírm and take héart.
Hópe in the Lórd!

■ d. Psalm 121

1. I rejoiced when I heard them say:
   'Let us go to God's house.'
   And now our feet are standing
   within your gates, O Jerusalem.

2. Jerusalem is built as a city
   strongly compact.
   It is there that the tribes go up,
   the tribes of the Lord.

3. For Israel's law it is,
   there to praise the Lord's name.
   There were set the thrones of judgement
   of the house of David.

4. For the peace of Jerusalem pray:
   'Peace be to your homes!
   May peace reign in your walls,
   in your palaces, peace!'

5. For love of my brethren and friends
   I say: 'Peace upon you!'
   For love of the house of the Lord
   I will ask for your good.

I rejóiced when I héard them sáy;
'Let us gó to God's hóuse.'
And nów our féet are stánding
within your gátes, O Jerúsalem.

Jerúsalem is búilt as a cíty
stróngly compáct.
It is thére that the tríbes go úp,
the tríbes of the Lórd.

For Ísrael's láw it ís,
there to práise the Lord's náme.
Thére were set the thrónes of júdgement
of the hóuse of Dávid.

For the péace of Jerúsalem práy:
'Péace be to your hómes!
May péace réign in your wálls,
in your pálaces, péace!'

For lóve of my bréthren and fríends
I say: 'Péace upon yóu!'
For lóve of the hóuse of the Lórd
I will ásk for your góod.

The reader must also take note and register the emotional content of the psalm. These are religious songs which express the full range of human experience; 'they are a series of shouts: shouts of love and hatred; shouts of suffering or rejoicing; shouts of faith or hope.'[14] The reader needs to communicate the emotional tone as well as the imagery which will help the assembly understand how the psalm is connected to the other pieces of scripture for that Sunday and to the liturgical season.

To do justice to the Psalm, you need to work with the text and rehearse as with any other scriptural selection. It is poetry and the assembly should sense this from the manner of its delivery, but it is also prayer and the assembly's response to the first reading. The reader should do everything possible to make that response strong.

2. Preparing readings from Paul's letters

The suggestions for working with text given under **Reflection** above are not really suitable with the second reading. This is because it is generally a kind of writing called **discourse** or **argument.** Here it is important to analyse the piece by first finding the key idea, and then identifying the logical structure which supports it. The second stage is careful proclamation, which means in general a much slower delivery so the listeners can grasp the different parts of the argument and how it progresses.

Before giving some exercises to work on, note should be taken of the **heading** which precedes every reading. What is its purpose? The *GIL* explains it thus:

> There is a *heading* prefixed to each text, chosen carefully (usually from the words of the text itself) in order to point out the main theme of the reading and, when necessary, to make the connection between the readings of the same Mass clear. [12.3]

In spite of this explanation the reader would be well-advised to take care, because it is not always the case that it points out the main theme. Look at the following passage from Galatians 1: 1-2, 6-10, for the 9th Sunday in Ordinary Time, Year C. The heading for the reading is: *If I still wanted men's approval, I should not be a servant of Christ.* With that in mind, read the passage, then look at the exercise opposite:

A reading from the letter of St Paul to the Galatians   1: 1-2. 6-10

If I still wanted men's approval, I should not be a servant of Christ.

From Paul to the churches of Galatia, and from all the brothers who are here with me, an apostle who does not owe his authority to men or his appointment to any human being but who has been appointed by Jesus Christ and by God the Father who raised Jesus from the dead. I am astonished at the promptness with which you have turned away from the one who called you and have decided to follow a different version of the God News. Not that there can be more than one Good News; it is merely that some troublemakers among you want to change the Good News of Christ; and let me warn you that if anyone preaches a version of the Good News different from the one we have already preached to you, whether it be ourselves or an angel from heaven, he is to be condemned. I am only repeating what we told you before: if anyone preaches a version of the Good News different from the one you have already heard, he is to be condemned. So now whom am I trying to please – man or God? Would you say it is men's approval I am looking for? If I still wanted that, I should not be what I am – a servant of Christ.

Exercise:

After reading the passage to yourself several times, answer the questions. It is best if you can work with others and compare your answers. The procedure can be used for all passages from St Paul; adapt it to those given below.

1) What is the main point of the salutation/first sentence?
2) What is the main point of the second paragraph?
   (Bear in mind that repetition is a device used to indicate importance.)
3) Would you say the heading is a good indication of the main point of this passage?
4) Are there any questions raised by the passage?
5) What mood was Paul in when he wrote this letter? (This should be reflected in the reader's voice when proclaiming the passage).
6) Decide where to breathe and which words to stress.
7) Practise the passage aloud until it feels comfortable.

a. A reading from the first letter of St Paul to the Corinthians   1: 22-25

Here we are preaching a crucified Christ, an obstacle to men, but to those who are called, the wisdom of God.

While the Jews demand miracles and the Greeks look for wisdom, here are we preaching a crucified Christ; to the Jews an obstacle that they cannot get over, to the pagans madness, but to those who have been called, whether they are Jews or Greeks, a Christ who is the power and the wisdom of God. For God's foolishness is wiser than human wisdom, and God's weakness is stronger than human strength.

3rd Sunday of Lent, year B

b. A reading from the letter of St Paul to Titus   2: 11-14. 3: 4-7

He saved us by the cleansing water of rebirth and by renewing us by the Holy Spirit.

God's grace has been revealed, and it has made salvation possible for the whole human race and taught us that what we have to do is to give up everything that does not lead to God, and all our worldly ambitions; we must be self-restrained and live good and religious lives here in this present world, while we are waiting in hope for the blessing which will come with the Appearing of the glory of our great God and saviour Christ Jesus. He sacrificed himself for us in order to set us free from all wickedness and to purify a people so that it would be his very own and would have no ambition except to do good.

When the kindness and love of God our saviour for mankind were revealed, it was not because he was concerned with any righteous actions we might have done ourselves; it was for no reason except his own compassion that he saved us, by means of the cleansing water of rebirth and by renewing us with the Holy Spirit which he has so generously poured over us through Jesus Christ our saviour. He did this so that we should be justified by his grace, to become heirs looking forward to inheriting eternal life.

The Baptism of the Lord, year C

c. A reading from the letter of St Paul to the Romans   6: 3-4. 8-11

When we were baptised we went into the tomb with Christ, so that we too might live a new life.

You have been taught that when we were baptised in Christ Jesus we were baptised in his death; in other words, when we were baptised we went into the tomb with him and joined him in death, so that as Christ was raised from the dead by the Father's glory, we too might live a new life.

But we believe that having died with Christ we shall return to life with him: Christ, as we know, having been raised from the dead will never die again. Death has no power over him any more. When he dierd, he died, once for all, to sin, so his life now is life with God; and in that way, you too must consider yourselves to be dead to sin but alive for God in Christ Jesus.

13th Sunday in Ordinary Time, year A

d. A reading from the letter to the Hebrews   4: 12-13

The word of God can judge secret emotions and thoughts.

The word of God is something alive and active: it cuts like any double-edged sword but more finely: it can slip through the place where the soul is divided from the spirit, or joints from the marrow; it can judge the secret emotions and thoughts. No created thing can hide from him; everything is uncovered and open to the eyes of the one to whom we must give account of ourselves.

28th Sunday in Ordinary Time, year B

3. The Book of Revelation (The Apocalypse)

Although readings from this book do not occur that often in the Sunday lectionary (only nine times in the three-year cycle), they are often the cause of dread for readers because they seem difficult to understand. With this book more than any other in the New Testament, it is important to understand the people for whom it was written and the times they lived in.

Apocalypse, the name used in the Lectionary, means 'revelation'. There is a wide variety of visionary writings in Jewish and Christian circles beginning from the time of the prophet Daniel at the end of the Old Testament. Chapters 7 to 12 of Daniel contain visionary dreams full of fantastic imagery which are interpreted by the angel Gabriel. It is a model followed by Revelation: both are addressed to a community suffering persecution and being put to death for their beliefs. Because of the times they lived in, they spoke in veiled language because criticism of their rulers was extremely dangerous: only those suffering with them would understand the meaning of the images they used. The present-day reader needs to set aside the literalness of our times and enter the world of those for whom the revelation was written.

The author tells us clearly who he is: a Christian prophet named John, living on the island of Patmos[16]. His revelation differs from his Jewish contemporaries:

'[John's vision] appears all at once, so that the reader is swept through scene after scene. Like an epic movie, these scenes are linked together with a dramatic sound track – the chaos and disorder of battle, the thunder of horses, the sound of trumpets, and the beautiful pauses in heaven when the heavenly hosts sing praises to God and to Christ. The onrush does not stop until we find ourselves in the peace of the new Jerusalem.'[17]

Although written for specific people (Christians living in Asia Minor) at a specific time (traditionally the reign of Domitian, assassinated in AD 96), Revelation deals with the serious question of how Christians are to live in a larger, often hostile society. Its message for Christians of that time is still relevant for us: we are warned against the temptation to be silent or look the other way in the presence of evil and injustice. No one is exempt from the obligation to bear witness.

Revelation was not written to frighten Christians into being good. Its purpose was and continues to be to encourage –

'when [evil] takes on all the trappings of divine, imperial power; when it also has the force of local opinion behind it; when even some religious leaders are lined up against the few who would resist. Yet, it is the faithful few who share the victory that Christ's death has won over evil.'[18]

With this in mind, the place to begin is to read the book through without stopping, even if we are not scheduled to read from it.

The Book of Revelation is the source of all the Second Readings on Sundays of Easter in Year C. Aside from this period of semi-continuous reading, the other occasions when we hear from John of Patmos are during the Chrism Mass, the feast of Christ the King in Year B, All Saints, and the Assumption.

While the readings in Year C are comprehensible without too much close study of the text, the assembly and all the readers would nevertheless benefit from a general introduction as the cycle begins, and this is recommended. However, the text which most find difficult either to proclaim or to understand is that for the Assumption.

A reading from the book of the Apocalypse   11: 19; 12: 1-6. 10

A woman adorned with the sun, standing on the moon.

Now a great sign appeared in heaven: a woman, adorned with the sun, standing on the moon, and with the twelve stars on her head for a crown. She was pregnant, and in labour, crying aloud in the pangs of childbirth. Then a second sign appeared in the sky, a huge red dragon which had seven heads and ten horns, and each of the seven heads crowned with a coronet. Its tail dragged a third of the stars from the sky and dropped them to the earth, and the dragon stopped in front of the woman as she was having the child, so that he could eat it as soon as it was born from its mother. The woman brought a male child into the world, the son who was to rule all the nations with an iron sceptre, and the child was taken straight up to God and to his throne, while the woman escaped into the desert, where God had made a place of safety ready. Then I heard a voice shout from heaven, 'Victory and power and empire for ever have been won by our God, and all authority for his Christ.'

To help with the proclaimer's understanding of this passage, here are commentaries from three useful sources.

a. From Aelred Rosser, *A Workbook for Lectors and Gospel Readers*

I'VE ALWAYS LOVED THE EPITAPH that Benjamin Franklin wrote for his own tomb:

The body of Benjamin Franklin, Printer (like the cover of an old book, its contents torn out and stripped of its lettering and gilding), lies here, food for worms; but the work shall not be lost, for it will (as he believed) appear once more in a new and more elegant edition, revised and corrected by the Author.

On the feast of Mary's assumption we are reminded that we are to follow her into glory, as she has folled Christ. We are reminded that what we call death is nothing more than the last thing we do in life. And it will be the best and finest thing we do, for in dying we are introduced into the presence of the one who conquered death. In Christ, death itself dies.

Mary had been taken up into heaven, body and soul. The promise brought to fulfillment in her is a promise we all share. Celebrating her triumph in Christ shbould give us pause, and it should give us hope as well. We pause to examine the fervour of this revolutionary belief, and we rejoice in the hope we receive from that belief.

The first reading is a classic example of apocalyptic literature in which metaphor and symbol are used to meditate on eternal truths. Mary has long been called 'ark of the covenant.' The woman clothed with the sun symbolizes at least three persons: the corporate person of Israel, triumphant in the fulfillment of God's promises; the church, through which the reign of God is expressed most vividly; and Mary, the mother of the Messiah, through whom the messianic promises were fulfilled and for whom a special place has been prepared.

Clearly the choice of this text for today's liturgy has the last of these three persons in mind, though not to the exclusion of the other two. The struggle between good and evil is personified in the woman and the dragon and the rescued child. Centuries of study have revealed that the various elements of this vision are taken from many sources. The drama presented here is effective on its own terms if it is read with confiction and great care.

b. From Dennis Hamm, *Let the Scriptures Speak*

A woman clothed with the sun

THE VISION OF the 'woman clothed with the sun, with the moon beneath her feet, and on her head a crown of twelve stars' (Rev 12: 1) is not first about Mary the mother of Jesus. In the context of Revelation, this figure, the best of Catholic biblical scholarship assures us, represents the People of God (old and new). The complex of sun, moon, and twelve stars figure in the dream of Joseph (Gen 37: 9-10, where sun and moon stand for his parents and eleven stars stand for his eleven brothers, all bowing down to him, the

twelfth). Woman Israel gives birth to the Messiah, after whose exaltation she continues to live (like Israel of the Exodus), endangered but divinely protected.

If the woman stands for the whole People of God, does that mean the Church's use of this text to honor Mary is biblically unwarranted? Not at all. First, the place of Mary in salvation history is surely implied in the reference to the birth of Israel's Messiah. Moreover, Mary the mother of Jesus is elsewhere treated in the Gospels as embodying the People of Israel. Indeed, the Gospel reading for this Sunday, the Magnificat, refers to the fuller history of Israel by echoing the hymn of Samuel's mother Hannah (1 Sam 2: 1-10), as well as seeing her (Mary's) motherhood as God's helping 'Israel his servant' and acting 'according to his promise…to Abraham and to his descendants forever' (Luke 1: 54-55). Thus, the liturgy's use of Revelation 12 to celebrate Mary is a most appropriate application of the text. Indeed, this appropria-tion brings about what is implicit in the text, Mary's place in God's history with Israel.

Today's first reading from Revelation further draws from Revelation by including a verse from the hymn in Revelation 12: 'Now have salvation and power come, / the kingdom of our God / and the authority of his Anointed.' Along with the selection from 1 Corinthians 15, this hymn places the Assumption in the fullest context. What was begun in Mary will come to fruition in nothing less than the fullness of the kingdom of God.

c. From Mary Birmingham, *Word and Worship Workbook*

THIS ESCHATOLOGICAL* READING reminds us of previous prophets who spoke of Jerusalem's and the people's promised glory in the last days. The image of a woman in the pangs of childbirth emerges as a symbol of new life that can come to pass only in the fullness of time and only after enduring unavoidable pain.

It is tempting to think that Mary is the mother about to give birth to Christ, the child about to be born. However, the author was not thinking of Mary. Christ is about to come to birth in the lives of people. It is painful because it is accompanied by sorrow, persecution, and the daily struggle to persevere. The woman is a symbol of the church who exists in the midst of God's glory, yet nevertheless is bound to the struggles of this earthly sojourn. Christ protects and strengthens her as she passes from death to life.

Even though the author of Revelation was not referring to Mary in his vision, Christian tradition has always understood the woman as an image of Mary.

The meaning is not changed, however. Mary is a symbol of the church who still gives birth to Christ in the lives of the faithful. 'God willed this unique and marvelous divine motherhood to be the figure and exemplar of the fecundity of the virgin Church that also becomes a mother… the Church in the sacrament of baptism somehow continues Mary's virginal motherhood. We may offer one example of this teaching from our predecessor St Leo the Great; in one of his Christmas sermons he says: '[Christ] placed in the baptismal font the source of his own origin in the womb of the Virgin: the power of the most high and the overshadowing of the water to give rebirth to the believer.' And if we want to find the same idea in liturgical sources we can cite the very beautiful *Illatio* [preface] of the Mozarabic liturgy: '[Mary] carried life in her womb; the Church, in the baptismal font. In the body of Mary Christ put on flesh; in the waters of the Church the baptized put on Christ.'

* Eschatological: dealing with the End Times or the Last Days.

From these commentaries it can be seen that it would be helpful to give a brief introduction to this reading on the Feast of the Assumption, explaining briefly the nature of the book of Revelation and an interpretation of the particular vision contained in the passage. This should be written down to ensure that it uses the fewest number of words while being clear. Of course, it should be shown to the presider for his agreement and approval. It should also be decided who will give the explanation, the presider or the reader. And then it should be proclaimed in a way that helps the assembly to see the vision with understanding.

PART THREE:
Ministry

The major part of this Workbook has focused on technical aspects of the reader's task. But it would not be complete without the reminder that this is above all a **ministry**, a service the reader gives to his/her community out of love of God.

This book and the Handbook before it operate from the outside-in because that is the way it works: we learn new skills and techniques from external sources and only after they have been mastered and internalized is it possible to consider them from the inside-out. But it is the internal changes, which only happen once they have become part of us, that will make the real transformation of our service. Thus these final remarks about ministry are the true heart of the matter. They are concerned with the spirituality of the reader and the importance of taking seriously the need to become holy.

There are many places where the reader can be directed to read about spirituality. Of all the possible sources, some suggestions from William J. Rademacher will be summarized here for their clarity and impact. They are found in *Lay Ministry: A Theological, Spiritual, and Pastoral Handbook* (St Paul Publications, 1991).

He begins by reminding us that ministry needs to be seen in the context of our baptismal consecration. Baptism was when the seed of holiness was planted, but its effects are not limited to this moment; the seed *grows* during the life of the minister.

There are several principles involved in developing a genuine spirituality for lay people. These relate to all ministers, but will here be applied specifically to readers.

1. Link the reader's call to holiness to the baptismal vocation. We are called to this state of holiness in our lives in the world; it is through us that Jesus continues to work in the world reconciling all people to the Father. The service we give as readers arises out of an awareness of the calling we share with all the baptized.

2. Nourish the spirit on the Bread of the Word. The reader becomes vulnerable and engages in a true dialogue with God through the Word. … Reflecting prayerfully on God's Word, hearing God's voice, is the life-blood of the spiritual life.' (p 193.) This is the first stage of the reader's preparation: it is essential, not only to make the proclamation better, but we can now see that it is indispensable in deepening the reader's connection with God. Rademacher quotes Martin Buber who explains that developing a relationship with God involves a summons and a sending. It will definitely change us. Therefore, if we are not prepared to change, or if we are not prepared to be sent, we ought never to go before the Word. (194)

3. Have an inner conviction about the centrality of the Jesus/Lord event as revealed in Scripture as the touchstone, 'testing the quality and genuineness of all forms of spirituality'. (195)

4. Be disposed to the ongoing conversion or change of heart which will follow our engagement with the Word. The message that is contained in the scripture passages each Sunday must have meaning for the reader first if it is to be proclaimed with conviction that will persuade and touch others. Of course, the Spirit is not dependent on the understanding of the reader, but part of ministry is the desire to cooperate as much as possible by giving voice to God's word.

5. Be compassionate. This means there is no escape from engagement with 'the pain and agony of this bent world' (195). Compassion means the ability to be present to others so that 'my capacity for hearing, seeing, feeling – indeed loving – is made available to another human being if for only a moment' (196). The reader recognizes that presence in the world means being Christ and bringing Christ to the places where he is needed. The strength to do this comes from the Bread of the Word.

6. Develop an awareness of the holiness of everyday things. We need to pause, often in the daily life to reflect on what is going on: the person who called by phone, the letter we received today, the beauty that is rushing past our car windows, the people we meet on the streets, the kiss we received and gave this morning, the illness we experience today, that article in the news about that child, this or that, all stuff from our everyday lives: we need to pause to notice it, reflect on it, let it touch us, let it move us. (cf. Bill Heubsch, *Spirituality of Wholeness,* Twenty-Third Publications, 1988, p 90).

7. Be open to contact with the Holy Spirit: awareness that the breath of God received at Baptism will continue to make ministry fruitful if the reader is open to receive it.

8. Understanding of the importance of 'holy time'. 'Unless we deliberately steal some "holy" time to commune with the Holy One, all our time will soon become "unholy" because we will become insensitive to, or unreflective about, the holy.' (p.198)

9. Moving towards holiness is moving toward wholeness. This happens as our spiritual lives become less and less complicated because the God we aspire to serve is simplicity.

With these principles in mind, what should be done, where should the reader begin? Here are three final suggestions which the reader will be able to use or supplement. They are: prayer; love of the liturgy; and the expectation and desire to change as a result of this ministry.

Prayer

The reader comes to this ministry out of a life of prayer. If this isn't already in place, steps should be taken to ensure that there is regular prayer which alone can help develop a deeper understanding of scripture. Before beginning to prepare a text, the reader prays to remind him/herself of dependence on God. Proclaiming scripture to the community is not an ego trip, but a form of service out of love of God which deserves the best the reader can do. The whole of the reader's preparation, the proclamation itself, and the review afterwards should all be seen as part of prayer.

Love of the liturgy

The reader develops a love of liturgy. There is an awareness of the structure of the liturgy and the importance of the liturgy of the word. The whole liturgy is understood as the work of all the assembly who give praise and thanksgiving to God for all the good things related and recalled in the scriptural passages. The reader understands that the liturgy is the source and summit of the Christian life:

> '…the **outstanding means** whereby the faithful may express in their lives and manifest to others the mystery of Christ and the real nature of the true Church',
> '…the source for achieving in **the most effective way possible** human sanctification and God's glorification, the end to which all the Church's other activities are directed…'   [CSL 10]

and also that

> the Church earnestly desires that all the faithful be led to that full, conscious, and active participation in liturgical celebration called for by the very nature of the liturgy, such participation by the Christian people is their right and duty by reason of their baptism, this full and active participation by all the people is the aim to be considered before all else. For it is the primary and indispensable source from which the faithful are to derive the true Christian spirit… [CSL 14]

Having grasped this and been convinced by it, the reader at liturgy (whether scheduled to read or not) should be a model of attention and involvement, not with this as the primary end in mind, but because s/he is compelled to this level of participation by the understanding of what is going on. Nothing done during the liturgy should be routine. From the time of entering the church, from the sign of the cross with holy water from the font, every action has meaning and should be done with care and attention.

Change as a result of ministry

Since the reader is so close to the word of God contained in scripture, there can be no escape from the message it conveys.

The first recommendation for improvement in this book (p.23) was a call for the reader to work and pray to find the meaning of the passage to his/her own life. This step will help the reader deliver the proclamation with conviction. But reading well is not an adequate response to scripture. The reader cannot be in such regular close contact with the word of God without being changed. The knowledge and preparation of God's word must go beyond the Sunday liturgy and be part of the readers' life. Proclaiming scripture well means that the reader struggles every day to become an example of the word of God in action. Being called to the ministry of the word should be under-stood and embraced as a call to discipleship, a call to demonstrate in our lives what we proclaim, to live out the values of our faith to be Christ in the world.

In closing: live the story

In closing, the reader's task can be summarized quite simply: it is to learn the story which s/he will proclaim, to love the story so that it can be brought to life for all listeners, and to live the story which is understood as a necessary part of our baptismal vocation. This last point is the heart of ministry. May God's blessings be on all who strive to do this.

APPENDIX A: Current Order of Readings

[Note: No indication of shortened readings is given in the following chart.]

This listing shows how the principle of semi-continuous reading of Gospels and the 2nd readings is worked out and provides a handy reference for the 1st readings, chosen to harmonise with the Gospel.

		YEAR A	YEAR B	YEAR C
ADVENT	1st Sunday	Isaiah 2: 1-5 Psalm 121 (122):1-2.4-9 Romans 13: 11-14 Matthew 24: 37-44	Isaiah 63: 16-17, 64: 1. 3-8 Psalm 1 Cor 1: 3-9 Mark 13: 33-37	Jeremiah 33: 14-16 Psalm 1 Thess 3: 12 – 4: 2 Luke 21: 25-28. 34-36
	2nd Sunday	Isaiah 11: 1-10 Psalm 71(72):1-2.7-8.12-13.17 Romans 15: 4-9 Matthew 3: 1-12	Isaiah 40: 1-5. 9-11 Psalm 2 Peter 3: 8-14 Mark 1: 1-8	Baruch 5: 1-9 Psalm Phil 1: 3-6. 8-11 Luke 3: 1-6
	3rd Sunday	Isaiah 35: 1-6.10 Psalm 145 (146):7-10 James 5: 7-10 Matthew 11: 2-11	Isaiah 61: 1-2. 10-11 Psalm 1 Thess 5: 16-24 John 1: 6-8. 19-28	Zeph 3: 14-18 Psalm Phil 4: 4-7 Luke 3: 10-18
	4th Sunday	Isaiah 7: 10-14 Psalm 23 (24)1-6 Romans 1: 1-7 Matthew 1: 18-24	2 Sam 7: 1-5. 8-12.14.16 Psalm Romans 16: 25-27 Luke 1: 26-38	Micah 5: 1-4 Psalm Hebrews 10: 5-10 Luke 1: 39-44
CHRISTMAS	Vigil Mass	Isaiah 62: 1-5 Psalm 88 (89):4-5.16-17.27.29 Acts 13: 16-17. 22-25 Matthew 1: 1-25		
	Midnight Mass	Isaiah 9: 1-7 Psalm 95 (96):1-3.11-13 Titus 2: 11-14 Luke 2: 1-14		
	Dawn Mass	Isaiah 62: 11-12 Psalm 96 (97):1.6.11-12 Titus 3: 4-7 Luke 2: 15-20		
	Day Mass	Isaiah 52: 7-10 Psalm 97 (97)1-6 Hebrews 1: 1-6 John 1: 1-18		
Sunday after Christmas	The Holy Family	Ecclesiasticus 3:2-6.12-14 Psalm 127 (128):1-5 Colossians 3:12-21 Matthew 2:13-15. 19-23	Genesis 15:1-6. 21:1-3 Psalm 104 (105):1-6. 8-9 Hebrews 11:8.11-12/ 17-19 Luke 2:22-40	1 Sam 1:20-22.24-28 Psalm 83(84):2-3. 5-6. 9-10 1 John 3:1-2.21-24 Luke 2:41-52
1 January	Solemnity of Mary	Numbers 6: 22-27 Psalm 66(67):2-3.5.6.8 Galatians 4: 4-7 Luke 2: 16-21		
	2nd Sunday after Christmas	Sirach 24: 1-2. 8-12 Psalm 147 Eph 1: 3-6. 15-18 John 1: 1-18		
6 January	Epiphany of the Lord	Isaiah 60: 1-6 Psalm 71(72)1-2. 7-8. 10-13 Eph 3: 2-3. 5-6 Matthew 2: 1-12		
Sunday after 6 January (Baptism of the Lord)		Isaiah 42: 1-4.6-7 Psalm 28(29):1-4. 9-10 Acts 10: 34-38 Matthew 3: 13-17	Isaiah 55:1-11 Isaiah 12:2-6 I John 5:1-9 Mark 1: 7-11	Isaiah 40:1-5. 9-11 Ps 103(104):1-2.3-4.24-25.27-30 Titus 2:11-14; 3:4-7 Luke 3: 15-16. 21-22

		YEAR A	YEAR B	YEAR C
LENT	Ash Wednesday	Joel 2:12-18 Psalm 50(51);3-6. 12-14. 17 2 Corinthians 5:20-6:2 Matthew 6:1-6. 16-18		
	1st Sunday	Gen 2: 7-9, 3: 1-7 Psalm 50(51);3-6. 12-14. 17 Rom 5: 12-19 Matthew 4: 1-11	Gen 9: 8-15 Psalm 24(25):4-9 1 Peter 3: 18-22 Mark 1: 12-15	Deut 26: 4-10 Psalm 90 (91):1-2.10-15 Romans 10: 8-13 Luke 4: 1-13
	2nd Sunday	Gen 12: 1-4 Psalm 32(33):4-5. 18-20. 22 2 Tim 1: 8-10 Matthew 17: 1-9	Gen 22: 1-2, 9,10-13,15-18 Psalm 115(116): 10.15-19 Rom 8: 31-34 Mark 9: 2-10	Gen 15: 5-12. 17-18 Psalm 26(27): 1.7-9. 13-14 Phil 3: 17-4:1 Luke 9: 28-36
	3rd Sunday	Exodus 17: 3-7 Psalm 94(95):1-2. 6-9 Rom 5: 1-2, 5-8 John 4: 5-42	Exodus 20: 1-17 Psalm 18(19): 8-11 1 Cor 1: 22-25 John 2: 13-25	Exodus 3: 1-8, 13-15 Psalm 102 (103: 1-4.6-8.11 1 Cor 10: 1-6, 10-12 Luke 13: 1-9
	4th Sunday	1 Sam 16: 1, 6-7, Psalm 22 (23) Eph 5: 8-14 John 9: 1-41	2 Chron 36: 14-16. 19-23 Psalm 136 (137) Eph 2: 4-10 John 3: 14-21	Joshua 5: 9, 10-12 Psalm 26(27):1. 7-9. 13-14 2 Cor 5: 17-21 Luke 15: 1-3, 11-32
	5th Sunday	Ezekiel 37: 12-14 Psalm 129(130) Rom 8: 8-11 John 11: 1-45	Jer 31: 31-34 Psalm 50(51):3-4.12-15 Hebrews 5: 7-9 John 12: 20-33	Isaiah 43: 16-21 Psalm 125(126) Phil 3: 8-14 John 8: 1-11
	Passion (Palm) Sunday	*Procession* Matthew 21: 1-11 *Mass for Years ABC* Isaiah 50: 4-7 Philippians 2: 6-11 Matthew 26: 14-27: 66	Mark 11: 1-10 Mark 14: 1-15: 47	Luke 19: 28-40 Luke 22: 14-23: 56
TRIDUUM Years ABC	Holy Thursday	Exodus 12: 1-8, 11-14; Psalm 115(116): 12-13. 15-18 1 Corinthians 11: 23-26 John 13: 1-15		
	Good Friday	Isaiah 52: 13 – 53: 12 Psalm 30(31): 2.6. 12-13. 15-17. 25 Hebrews 4: 14-16, 5: 7-9 John 18: 1 – 19: 42		
	Easter Vigil	Genesis 1: 1 – 2: 2; Ps 103 (104)1-2. 5.6. 10.12-14. 24. 35 *or* 32(33):4-7.12-13. 20.22 Genesis 22: 1-18; Psalm 15(16): 5.8-11 Exodus 14: 15 – 15: 1; [Canticle] Exodus 15:1-6. 17-18 Isaiah 54: 5-14; Psalm 29(30): 2.4-6.11-13 Isaiah 55: 1-11; [Canticle] Isaiah 12:2-6 Baruch 3: 9-15, 32 – 4: 4; Psalm 18(19): 8-11 Ezekiel 36: 16-17, 18-28; Ps 41(42):3,5; 42(43) 3,4; *if there is a baptism* Is 12:2-6 or Psalm 50(51)12.15.18.19 may be used instead Romans 6: 3-1; Psalm 117(118):1-2. 16-17. 22-23		
		Matthew 28: 1-10	Mark 16: 1-7	Luke 24: 1-12
	Easter Sunday	Acts 10: 34, 37-43 Psalm 117(118): 1-2. 16-17. 22-23 Colossians 3: 1-4 **or** 1 Cor 5: 6-8 John 20: 1-9 (Evening: Luke 24: 13-35)		
EASTER SEASON	2nd Sunday of Easter	Acts 2: 42-47 Ps 117(118):1-2. 13-15. 22-24 1 Peter 1: 17-21 John 20: 19-31	Acts 4: 32-35 117(118):2-4. 15-18. 22-24 1 John 5: 1-6 John 20: 19-31	Acts 5: 12-16 117(118):2-4. 22-27 Rev 1: 9-11, 12-13, 17-19 John 20: 19-31

		YEAR A	YEAR B	YEAR C
	3rd Sunday of Easter	Acts 2: 14, 22-33 Psalm 15(16):2.5.7-11 1 Peter 1: 17-21 Luke 24: 13-35	Acts 3: 13-15, 17-19 Psalm 4: 2.4.7.9 1 John 2: 1-5 Luke 24: 35-48	Acts 5: 27-32, 40-41 Psalm 29)30):2.4-6.11-13 Rev 5: 11-14 John 21: 1-19
	4th Sunday of Easter	Acts 2: 14, 36-41 Psalm 22(23) 1 Peter 2: 20-25 John 10: 1-10	Acts 4: 8-12 117(118):1.8-9.21-23.26.28-29 1 John 3: 1-2 John 10: 1-10	Acts 13: 14, 43-52 Psalm 99(100:1-3.5 Rev 7: 9, 14-17 John 10: 27-30
	5th Sunday of Easter	Acts 6: 1-7 Psalm 32(33):1-2.4-5.18-19 1 Peter 2: 4-9 John 14: 1-12	Acts 9: 26-31 Ps 21(22):26-28/ 30-32 1 John 3: 18-24 John 15: 1-18	Acts 14: 21-27 Psalm 144:8-13 Rev 21: 1-5 John 13: 32-33, 34-35
	6th Sunday of Easter	Acts 8: 5-8, 14-17 Psalm 65(66):1-7.16.20 1 Peter 3: 15-18 John 14: 15-21	Acts 10: 25-26,34-35, 44, 48 Psalm 97(98):1-4 1 John 4: 7-10 John 15: 9-17	Acts 15: 1-2, 22-29 Psalm 66(67):2-3.5-6.8 Rev 21: 10-14, 22-23 John 14: 23-29
	Ascension Thursday	Acts 1: 1-11 Psalm 46(47):2-3.6-9 Eph 1: 17-23 Matthew 28: 16-20	 Eph 4: 1-13 Mark 16: 15-20	 Heb 9: 24-28, 10: 19-23 Luke 24: 46-53
	7th Sunday of Easter	Acts 1: 12-14 Psalm 26(27):1.4.7-8 1 Peter 4: 13-16 John 17: 1-11	Acts 1: 15-17, 20,-26 Ps 102(103):1-2.11-12.19-20 1 John 4: 11-16 John 17: 11-19	Acts 7: 55-60 Psalm 96(97):1-2.6-7.9 Rev 22: 12-14, 16-17, 20 John 17: 20-26
	Pentecost Sunday	Acts 2: 1-11 Psalm 103(104): 1.24-29-31 1 Cor 12: 3-7, 12-13 John 20: 19-23	 Gal 5: 16-25 John 15: 26-27, 16: 12-15	 Romans 8: 8-17 John 14: 15-16, 23-26
	Trinity Sunday	Ex 34: 4-6, 8-9 Psalm: Dan 3:52-56 2 Cor 13: 11-13 John 3: 16-18	Deut 4: 32-34, 39-40 Psalm 32:4-6.9.18-20.22 Romans 8: 14-17 Matthew 28: 16-20	Proverbs 8: 22-31 Psalm 8:4-9 Romans 5: 1-5 John 16: 12-15
	The Body & Blood of Christ	Deut 8:2-3.14-16 Psalm 147:12-15 1 Cor 10:16-17 John 6:51-58	Exodus 24:3-8 Ps 115(116):12-13.15-18 Hebrews 9:11-15 Matrk 14:12-16.22-26	Genesis 14:18-20 Psalm 109(110):1-4 1 Cor 11:23-26 Luke 9:11-17
ORDINARY TIME	2nd Sunday	Isaiah 49: 3, 5-6 Psalm 39(40):2.4.7-10 1 Cor 1: 1-3 John 1: 29-34	1 Samuel 3: 3-10, 19 Psalm 39(40):2.4.7-10 1 Cor 6: 13-15, 17-20 John 1: 35-41	Isaiah 62: 1-5 Psalm 95(96): 1-3.7-10 1 Cor 12: 4-11 John 2: 1-11
	3rd Sunday	Isaiah 8: 23-9:3 Psalm 26(27): 1.4.13-14 1 Cor 1: 10-13, 17 Matthew 4: 12-23	Jonah 3: 1-5, 10 Psalm 24(25): 4-9 1 Cor 7: 29-31 Mark 1: 14-20	Neh 8: 2-4, 5-6, 8-10 Psalm 18(19): 8-10.15 1 Cor 12: 12-30 Luke 1: 1-4; 4: 14-21
	4th Sunday	Zeph 2: 3; 3: 12-13 Psalm 145(146): 7-10 1 Cor 1: 26-31 Matthew 5: 1-12	Deut 18: 15-20 Psalm 94(95): 1-2.6-9 1 Cor 7: 32-35 Mark 1: 21-28	Jer 1: 4-5, 17-19 Psalm 70(71):1-6.15.17 1 Cor 12: 31-13: 13 Luke 4: 21-20
	5th Sunday	Isaiah 58: 7-10 Psalm 111(112): 4-9 1 Cor 2: 1-5 Matthew 5: 13-16	Job 7: 1-4, 6-7 Psalm 146:1-6 1 Cor 9: 16-19, 22-23 Mark 1: 29-39	Isaiah 6: 1-2, 3-8 Psalm 137(138): 1-5. 7-8 1 Cor 15: 1-11 Luke 5: 1-11
	6th Sunday	Sirach 15: 15-20 Ps 118(119):1-2.4-5.17-18.33-34 1 Cor 2: 6-10 Matthew 5: 17-37	Lev 13: 1-2, 44-46 Psalm 31(32): 1-2.5.11 2 Cor 1: 18-22 Mark 1: 40-45	Jer 17: 5-8 Psalm 1:1-4.6 1 Cor 12, 16-20 Luke 6: 17, 20-26
	7th Sunday	Lev 19: 1-2, 17-18 Ps 102(103):1-4.8.10.12-13 1 Cor 3: 16-23 Matthew 5: 38-48	Isaiah 43: 18-19.21-22. 24-25 Psalm 40(41):2-5.13-14 2 Cor 1: 18-22 Mark 2: 1-12	1 Sam 26: 2, 7-9, 12-13, 22-23 Ps 102(103):1-4.8.10.12-13 1 Cor 15: 45-49 Luke 6: 27-38

ORDINARY TIME	YEAR A	YEAR B	YEAR C
8th Sunday	Isaiah 49: 14-15 Psalm 61(62):2-3.6-9 1 Cor 4: 1-5 Matthew 6: 24-34	Hosea 2: 16, 17, 21-22 Ps 102(103):1-4.8.10.12-13 2 Cor 3: 1-6 Mark 2: 18-22	Sirach 27: 4-7 Psalm 95(96):1-3.7-10 1 Cor 15: 54-58 Luke 6: 39-45
9th Sunday	Deut 11: 18. 26-28. 32 Psalm 30(31):2-4.17.25 Romans 3: 21-25. 28 Matthew 7: 21-27	Deut 5: 12-15 Psalm 80(81): 3-8.10-11 2 Cor 4: 6-11 Mark 2: 23 – 3: 6	1 Kings 8: 41-43 Psalm 116(117) Gal 1: 1-2. 6-10 Luke 7: 1-10
10th Sunday	Hosea 6: 3-6 Psalm 49(50): 1.8.12-15 Romans 4: 18-25 Matthew 9: 9-13	Genesis 3: 9-15 Psalm 129(130) 2 Cor 4: 13 – 5: 1 Mark 3: 20-35	1 Kings 17: 17-24 Psalm 29(30): 4-6.11-13 Gal 1: 11-19 Luke 7: 11-17
11th Sunday	Exodus 19: 2-6 Psalm 99(100): 2-3. 5 Romans 5: 6-11 Matthew 9: 36 – 10: 8	Ezekiel 17: 22-24 Psalm 91(92):2-3.13-16 2 Cor 5: 6-10 Mark 4: 26-34	2 Samuel 12: 7-10. 13 Psalm 31(32): 1-2.5.7.11 Gal 2: 16. 19-21 Luke 7: 36 – 8: 3
12th Sunday	Jer 20: 10-13 Ps 68(69): 8-10.14.17.33-35 Romans 5: 12-15 Matthew 10: 26-33	Job 38: 1, 8-11 Ps106(107): 23-26.28-31 2 Cor 5: 14-17 Mark 4: 35-41	Zech 12: 10-11, 13: 1 Psalm 62(63): 2-6.8-9 Gal 3: 26-29 Luke 9: 18-24
13th Sunday	2 Kings 4: 8-11, 14-16 Psalm 88(89): 2-3. 16-19 Romans 6: 3-4, 8-11 Matthew 10: 37-42	Wisdom 1: 13-15, 2: 23-24 Psalm 29(30):2.4-6.11-13 2 Cor 89: 7, 9, 13-15 Mark: 5: 21-43	1 Kings 19: 16, 19-21 Psalm 15(16): 1-2.5.7-11 Gal 5: 1, 13-18 Luke 9: 51-62
14th Sunday	Zech 9: 9-10 Ps 144(145):1-2.8-11.13-14 Romans 8: 9, 11-13 Matthew 11: 25-30	Ezekiel 2: 2-5 Psalm 122(123) 2 Cor 12: 7-10 Mark 6: 1-6	Isaiah 66: 10-14 Psalm 65(66):1-7.16.20 Gal 6: 14-18 Luke 10: 1-12, 17-20
15th Sunday	Isaiah 55: 10-11 Psalm 64(65): 10-14 Romans 8: 18-23 Matthew 13: 1-23	Amos 7: 12-15 Psalm 84(85): 9-14 Eph 1: 3-14 Mark 6: 7-13	Deut 30: 10-14 Psalm 68(69) or Ps 18 (19) Col 1: 15-20 Luke 10: 25-37
16th Sunday	Wisdom 12: 13, 16-19 Psalm 85(86): 5-6.9-10.15-16 Romans 8: 26-27 Matthew 13: 24-43	Jeremiah 23: 1-6 Psalm 22(23) Eph 2: 13-18 Mark 6: 30-34	Genesis 18: 1-10 Psalm 14(15): 2-5 Col 1: 24-28 Luke 10: 38-42
17th Sunday	1 Kings 3: 5, 7-12 Ps 118(119): 57.72.76-77.127-130 Romans 8: 28-30 Matthew 13: 44-52	2 Kings 4: 42-44 Ps 144(145): 10-11.15-18 Ephesians 4: 1-6 John 6: 1-15	Genesis 18: 20-32 Psalm 137(138) Col 2: 12-14 Luke 11: 1-13
18th Sunday	Isaiah 55: 1-3 Psalm 144(145):8-9.15-18 Romans 8: 35, 37-39 Matthew 14: 13-21	Exodus 16: 2-4, 12-15 Psalm 77(79):3-4.23-25.54 Eph 4: 17, 20-24 John 6: 24-35	Eccl 1: 2, 2: 21-23 Psalm 89(90) or Ps 94(95) Col 3: 1-5, 9-11 Luke 12: 13-21
19th Sunday	1 Kings 19: 9, 11-13 Psalm 84(85): 9-14 Romans 9: 1-5 Matthew 14: 22-23	1 Kings 19: 4-8 Psalm 33(34): 2-9 Eph 4: 30-52 John 6: 41-51	Wisdom 18: 6-9 Psalm 32(33): 1.12.18-20.22 Heb 11: 1-2, 8-19 Luke 12: 32-48
20th Sunday	Isaiah 56: 1, 6-7 Psalm 66(67): 2-3.5-6.8 Rom 11: 13-15, 29-32 Matthew 15: 21-28	Proverbs 9: 1-6 Psalm 33(34): 2-3.10-15 Eph 5: 15-20 John 6: 51-58	Jer 38: 4-6, 8-10 Psalm 39(40): 2-4.18 Hebrews 12: 1-4 Luke 12: 49-53
21st Sunday	Isaiah 22: 19-23 Psalm 137(138): 1-3.6.8 Romans 11: 33-36 Matthew 16: 13-20	Joshua 24: 1-2, 15-18 Psalm 33(34): 2-3.16-23 Eph 5: 21-32 John 6: 60-69	Isaiah 66: 18-21 Psalm 116(117) Heb 12: 5-7, 11-13 Luke 12: 22-30
22nd Sunday	Jer 20: 7-9 Psalm 62(63): 2-6.8-9 Romans 12: 1-2 Matthew 16: 21-27	Deut 4: 1-2, 6-8 Psalm 14(15): 2-5 Jam 1: 17-18, 21-22, 27 Mark 7: 108, 14-15,	Sir 3: 17-18, 20, 28-29 Psalm 67 (68):4-7.10-11 Heb 12: 18-19, 22-24 Luke 14: 1, 7-14.21-23

ORDINARY TIME	YEAR A	YEAR B	YEAR C
23rd Sunday	Ezekiel 33: 7-9 Psalm 94(95): 1-2.6-9 Romans 13: 8-10 Matthew 18: 15-20	Isaiah 35: 4-7 Psalm 145:7-10 James 2: 1-5 Mark 8: 27-35	Wisdom 9: 13-19 Psalm 89(90): 3-6.12-14.17 Phil 9-10, 12-17 Luke 14: 25-33
24th Sunday	Sirach 27: 33-28: 9 Psalm 102(103): 1-4.9-12 Romans 14: 7-9 Matthew 18: 21-35	Isaiah 50: 5-9 Psalm 114(115): 1-6.8-9 James 2: 14-18 Mark 8: 27-35	Exodus 32: 7-11, 13-14 Ps 50(51): 3-4.12-13.17.19 1 Tim 1: 12-17 Luke 15: 1-32
25th Sunday	Isaiah 55: 6-9 Ps 144(145):1-3.8-9.17-18 Phil 1: 20-24, 27 Matthew 20: 1-6	Wisdom 2: 12, 17-20 Psalm 53(54): 3-6.8 James 3: 16-4: 3 Mark 9: 30-37	Amos 8: 4-7 Psalm 112(113): 1-2.4-8 1 Tim 2: 108 Luke 16: 1-13
26th Sunday	Ezekiel 18: 25-28 Psalm 24(25): 4-9 Phil 2: 1-11 Matthew 21: 28-32	Numbers 11: 25-29 Psalm 18(19): 8.10.12-14 James 5: 1-6 Mark 9: 38-43, 45, 47-48	Amos 6: 1, 4-7 Psalm 145(146): 6-10 1 Tim 6: 11-16 Luke 16: 19-31
27th Sunday	Isaiah 5: 1-7 Psalm 79(80): 9.12-16.19-20 Phil 4: 6-9 Matthew 21: 33-43	Gen 2: 18-24 Psalm 127(128) Hebrews 2: 9-11 Mark 10: 2-16	Habbakuk 1: 2-3, 2: 2-4 Psalm 94(95): 1-2.6-9 2 Tim 1: 6-8, 13-14 Luke 17: 5-10
28th Sunday	Isaiah 25: 6-10 Psalm 22(23) Phil 4: 12-14, 19-20 Matthew 1-14	Wisdom 7: 7-11 Psalm 89(90): 12-17 Hebrews 4: 12-13 Mark 10: 17-30	2 Kings 5: 14-17 Psalm 97(98): 1-4 2 Tim 2: 8-13 Luke 17: 11-19
29th Sunday	Isaiah 45: 1, 4-6 Psalm 95(96)Ú 1.3-5.7-10 1 Thess 1: 5-10 Matthew 22: 15-21	Isaiah 53: 10-11 Ps 32(33):4-5.18-20.22 Hebrews 4: 14-16 Mark 10: 35-45	Exodus 17: 8-13 Psalm 120(121) 2 Tim 3: 14-4: 2 Luke 18: 1-8
30th Sunday	Exodus 22: 20-26 Psalm 17(18): 2-4.47.51 1 Thes 1: 5-10 Matthew 22: 34-40	Jeremiah 31: 7-9 Psalm 125(126) Hebrews 5: 1-6 Mark 10: 46-52	Sirach 35: 12-14, 16-18 Psalm 32(33): 2-3.17-19.23 2 Tim 4: 6-8, 16-18 Luke 18: 9-14
31st Sunday	Mal 1: 14 – 2: 2. 8-10 Psalm 130(131) 1 Thess 2: 7-9. 13 Matthew 23: 1-12	Deut 6: 2-6 Psalm 17(18):2-4.47.51 Hebrews 7: 23-28 Mark 12: 28-34	Wisdom 11: 22 – 12: 2 Ps 144(145):1-2.8-11.13-14 2 Thess 1: 11 – 2: 2 Luke 19: 1-10
32nd Sunday	Wisdom 6: 12-16 Psalm 62(63): 2-8 1 Thes 4: 13-18 Matthew 25: 1-13	1 Kings 17: 10-16 Psalm 145(146): 7-10 Hebrews 9: 24-28 Mark 12: 38-44	1 Maccabees 7: 1-2. 9-14 Psalm 16(17):1.5-6.8.15 2 Thess 2: 16 – 3: 5 Luke 20: 27-38
33rd Sunday	Prov 31: 10-13.19-20.30-31 Psalm 127(128): 1-5 1 Thess 5: 1-6 Matthew 25: 14-30	Daniel 12: 1-13 Psalm 15(16): 5.8-11 Hebrews 10: 11-14. 18 Mark 13: 24-32	Malachi 3: 19-20 Psalm 97(98): 5-9 2 Thess 3: 7-12 Luke 21: 5-19

Last Sunday in Ordinary Time: Our Lord Jesus Christ, Universal King

	YEAR A	YEAR B	YEAR C
	Ezekiel 34: 11-12. 15-17 Psalm 22(23): 1-3.5-6 1 Cor 15: 20-26. 28 Matthew 25: 31-46	Daniel 7: 13-14 Psalm 92(93): 1-2.5 Apoc 1: 5-8 John 18: 33-37	2 Samuel 5: 1-3 Psalm 121(122): 1-5 Col 1: 12-20 Luke 23: 35-42

APPENDIX B

Exercises for use in preparing scriptural texts

Contents of Appendix B: 1: General Articulation; B: Pauses and Phrasing (p.50); 3: Word Stress (p.51); 4: Word Colour (p.52); 5: Active Words (p.53); 6: Quotations (p.55); 7: Repetition and Balance (p.56)

The material used in this section is adapted from Ray Longergan's *A Workbook for Lectors: A Well-Trained Tongue*, Liturgy Training Publications, 1982. The extracts given here provide texts which can be used in working on various aspects of public speaking. Each section has an explanatory section before the passages.

1. General articulation

a. Peter Piper, the pepper picker, picked a peck of pickled peppers. A peck of pickled peppers did Peter Piper, the pepper picker, pick. If Peter Piper, the pepper picker, picked a peck of pickled peppers, where is the peck of pickled peppers that Peter Piper, the pepper picker, picked?

b. Swan, swim over the sea.
Swim, swan, swim!
Swan, swim back again.
Well swam, swan!

c. On two thousand acres, too tangled for tilling,
Where thousands of thorn trees grew thrifty and thrilling,
Theophilus Twistle, less thrifty than some,
Thrust three thousand thistles through the thick of his thumb!

d. When does the wristwatch strap shop shut?
Does the wristwatch strap shop shut soon?
Which wristwatch straps are Swiss wristwatch straps?

e. An icehouse ... not a nice house.
The summer school ... not a summer's cool.
Your two eyes ... not you're too wise.
Five minutes to eight ... not five minutes to wait.
Give me some ice ... not some mice.
His acts ... not his axe.

2. Pauses and phrasing

In preparing the text, the reader needs to read in a way that makes the meaning clear to the listener. An important way of doing this is by the use of pauses, either before an important word or after it, and by phrasing: making thought patterns clear by pausing after each related group. Deciding where the phrases are and therefore where to place pauses is important with any text, but especially with challenging ones like the letters of St Paul.

Look at each of the three texts which follow and decide where the pauses should be. It's useful to remember that there are short pauses (within a sentence) and longer ones signalled by the use of a full stop in the text. The reader needs to find a balance between making the ideas in the passage clear and putting in too many pauses which will lead to a choppy delivery.

a.   A reading from the letter of Paul to the Romans   1: 1-7

From Paul, a servant of Christ Jesus who has been called to be an apostle, and specially chosen to preach the Good News that God promised long ago through his prophets in the scriptures.

This news is about the Son of God, who, according to the human nature he took, was a descendant of David: it isabout Jesus Chist our Lord who, in the order of the spirit, the spirit of holiness that was in him, was proclaimed Son of God in al his power through his resurrection from the dead. Through him we received grace and our apostolic mission to preach the obedience of faith to all pagan nations in honour of his name. You are one of these nations, and by his call belong to Jesus Christ. To you all, then, who are God's beloved in Rome, called to be saints, may God our Father and the Lord Jesus Christ send grace and peace.

(4th Sunday of Advent, Year A)

b.   A reading from the first letter of Paul to the Thessalonians   5: 16-24

Be happy at all times; pray constantly; and for all things give thanks to God, because this is what God expects you to do in Christ Jesus.

Never try to suppress the Spirit or treat the gift of prophecy with contempt; think before you do anything – hold on to what is good and avoid every form of evil.

May the God of peace make you perfect and holy; and may you all be kept safe and blameless, spirit, soul and body, for the coming of our Lord Jesus Chrsit. God has called you and he will not fail you.

(RCIA: Rite of Reception into Full Communion: Lectionary Vol. III, p.78)

c. A reading from the book of Genesis   15: 5-12, 17-18

God took Abram outside and said, 'Look up to heaven and count the stars if you can. Such will be your descendants' he told him. Abram put his faith in the Lord, who counted this as making him justified.

'I am the Lord,' he said to him, 'who brought you out of Ur of the Chaldaeans to make you heir to this land.' 'My Lord God,' Abram replied, 'How am I to know that I shall inherit it?' He said to him, 'Get me a three-year-old heifer, a three-year-old goat, a three-year-old ram, a turtledove and a young pigeon.' He brought him all these, cut them in half and put half on one side and half facing it on the other; but the birds he did not cut in half. Birds of prey came down on the carcasses but Abram drove them off.

Now as the sun was setting Abram fell into a deep sleep, and terror seized him.

When the sun had set and darkness had fallen, there appeared a smoking furnace and a firebrand that went between the halves. That day the Lord made a Covenant with Abram in these terms:

'To your descendants I give this land, from the
Wadi of Egypt to the Great river, the river Euphrates.'

(1st Reading for the2nd Sunday of Lent, Year C)

3. Word stress

When speaking to someone, we show which words are important by stressing them – giving them extra weight, underlining them with our voice. This improves communication by giving the listener clues about what we mean and what is important in what we are saying.

The first passage is marked showing the suggested stress by *italicising* the stressed word. This is only a suggestion and is not to be considered obligatory, but it may help in showing how to work with text.

a. A reading from the book of the prophet Amos   7: 12-15

Amaziah, the priest of *Bethel*, said to *Amos*,
'O *seer*, *go*, flee *away* to the land of *Judah*,
earn your bread *there*, and prophesy *there;*
but never *again* prophesy at *Bethel*, for it is the king's *sanctuary*,
and it is a *temple* of the *kingdom*.'
Then Amos *answered* Amaziah,
'I am no *prophet*, nor a prophet's *son;*
but I am a *herdsman*, and a dresser of *sycamore* trees,
and the Lord *took* me from following the *flock*,
and the Lord *said* to me,
"*Go, prophesy* to my people *Israel*." '

(NRSV translation. 1st Reading of the 15th Sunday in Ordinary Time, Year B)

The next passage shows how to *overdo* it. Try reading the passage aloud, leaning on the underlined words, and suggest what changes you would make.

b. A reading from the first letter of Paul to the Corinthians 6: 13c-15a. 17-20

The body is <u>not</u> for immortality; <u>it</u> is for the <u>Lord</u>, and the <u>Lord</u> is for the <u>body</u>. <u>God</u>, who <u>raised</u> up the <u>Lord</u>, will raise us also by his <u>power</u>. Do <u>you</u> not <u>see</u> that your <u>bodies</u> are <u>members</u> of Christ? Whoever is <u>joined</u> to the Lord becomes <u>one spirit</u> with him. Shun <u>lewd</u> conduct. Every <u>other</u> sin a man commits is <u>outside</u> his body, but the fornicator <u>sins</u> against his <u>own body</u>. <u>You</u> must know that your <u>body</u> is a <u>temple</u> of the Holy Spirit, who is <u>within</u> – the <u>Spirit</u> you have received from <u>God</u>. You are not your <u>own</u>. <u>You</u> have been purchased, and <u>at</u> what a price! So <u>glorify</u> God in your <u>body</u>.

(New American Bible version. 2nd Reading of the 2nd Sunday in Ordinary Time, Year B.)

Now mark the stress in the following passage.

c. A reading from the first letter of Paul to the Thessalonians 5: 16-24

Be happy at all times; pray constantly; and for all things give thanks to God, because this is what God expects you to do in Christ Jesus.

Never try to suppress the Spirit or treat the gift of prophecy with contempt; think before you do anything – hold on to what is good and avoid every form of evil.

May the God of peace make you perfect and holy; and may you all be kept safe and blameless, spirit, soul, and body, for the coming of our Lord Jesus Christ. God has called you, and he will not fail you.

(2nd Reading of the 3rd Sunday of Advent, Year B.)

4. Word colour

Some words in any passage require special attention because they express a meaning important to the sentence, or an attitude or feeling which affects the whole passage. Look at the following examples . Say them aloud and try to let your voice convey the meaning of the underlined word.

a. A <u>child</u> is born to us, a <u>son</u> is given to us.
b. You are no longer a <u>slave</u>, but a <u>son</u>.
c. Jesus said to his disciples, "I have come to light a <u>fire</u> on the earth."
d. God's word is <u>living</u> and <u>effective</u>, <u>sharper</u> than a two-edged sword.
e. Speak <u>tenderly</u> to Jerusalem.
f. Your wealth has <u>rotted</u>…your gold and silver have <u>corroded</u>.

It will become clear that 'word colour' has to do with the *voice* of the reader. To do this well requires first visualising the effect desired and then working to achieve it. Also involved here are aspects like the *pitch* of the voice – the vocal range covered. In general, most readers could extend their vocal range with good effect.

5. Active words

The words here are usually verbs or verb forms which convey action. Visualise each of the following actions and then say the words aloud in a way that expresses the action. Do the same with the sentences that follow.

strike   caress   plead   sprinkle   bloom   elevate

a. The Lord let his face <u>shine</u> upon you.

b. He <u>prunes</u> away every barren branch, but the fruitful ones he <u>trims</u> clean to <u>increase</u> their yield.

c. It will <u>devour</u> your flesh like a fire.

d. Mary <u>treasured</u> all these things and <u>reflected</u> on them in her heart.

e. I <u>gave</u> my back to those who <u>beat</u> me, my cheeks to those who <u>plucked</u> my beard.

f. You <u>condemned</u>, even <u>killed</u> the just man.

g. God's word <u>penetrates</u> and <u>divides</u> soul and spirit...it <u>judges</u> the reflections and thoughts of the heart.

h. He did not deem equality with God something to be <u>grasped</u> at. Rather he <u>emptied</u> himself and took the form of a slave, being born in the likeness of men.

Below is one of the most challenging and beautiful texts in the Lectionary. It is a vision of the promise of the Second Coming, read during Advent in Year A. This is a painting in words. The reader first needs to understand the text by identifying the different sections, to find the high point and what leads up to it. Once this is done, the reader has to work out a way to proclaim it to help the assembly visualise the picture it paints. A suggested analysis follows.

A reading from the book of the prophet Isaiah   35: 1-6.10

Let the wilderness and the dry-lands exult,
let the wasteland rejoice and bloom,
let it bring forth flowers like the jonquil,
let it rejoice and sing for joy.

The glory of Lebanon is bestowed on it,
the splendour of Carmel and Sharon;
they shall see the glory of the Lord,
the splendour of our God.

Strengthen all weary hands,
steady all trembling knees
and say to all faint hearts,
'Courage! Do not be afraid.

'Look, your God is coming,
vengeance is coming,

the retribution of God;
he is coming to save you.

Then the eyes of the blind shall be opened,
The ears of the deaf unsealed,
Then the lame shall leap like a deer
And the tongues of the dumb sing for joy;
For those the Lord has ransomed shall return.

They will come to Zion shouting for joy,
Everlasting joy on their faces;
Joy and gladness will go with them
And sorrow and lament be ended.

Suggested analysis

This is one way (not the *only* way) in which the text can be analysed to highlight its structure. Understanding the shape of the passage and paying attention to the important action words will help the reader feel comfortable with it.

Start small and build to mid- plateau, while being careful with action words.

Let the wilderness and the dry-lands **exult**,
let the wasteland **rejoice** and **bloom**,
let it bring forth flowers like the jonquil,
let it **rejoice** and **sing** for joy.

The glory of Lebanon is **bestowed** on it,
the splendour of Carmel and Sharon;
they shall **see** the glory of the Lord,
the splendour of our God.

PAUSE here ➡

Make every verb in this section count,

Strengthen all weary hands,
steady all trembling knees
and say to all faint hearts,

building to this phrase: ➡

'Courage! Do not be afraid.

'Look, your God is coming,
vengeance is coming,
the retribution of God;
he is coming to save you.

PAUSE here ➡

Begin at lower level and build carefully.

Then the eyes of the blind shall be **opened**,
The ears of the deaf **unsealed**,
Then the lame shall **leap** like a deer
And the tongues of the dumb **sing** for joy;

Peak phrase: ➡

This is the closing part, on a lower level than preceding section, but satisfying.

For those the Lord has ransomed shall **return**.
They will come to Zion **shouting** for joy,
Everlasting joy on their faces;
Joy and gladness will go with them
And sorrow and lament be **ended**.

6. Quotations

There are two important situations in which quotations appear: In scriptural passages where there is dialogue between two or more people, and where there is an excerpt from the Old Testament included in the text. In both the reader has to make clear to the assembly what is happening.

The only way to do this vocally is to set off the quotes by sizable pauses both before and after. The reader should also make clear the coherence of the quoted passage. In this way, the listening ear can distinguish the quote as well as the eye can while reading.

Below are three passages containing quotes which can be used for practice.

a. A reading from the Acts of the Apostles   7: 55 – 8:1a

Stephen, filled with the Holy Spirit, gazed into heaven and saw the glory of God, and Jesus standing at God's right hand. 'I can see heaven thrown open,' he said, 'and the Son of Man standing at the right hand of God.' At this all the members of the council shouted out and stopped their ears with their hands; then they all rushed at him, sent him out of the city and stoned him. The witnesses put down their clothes at the feet of a young man called Saul. As they were stoning him, Stephen said in invocation, 'Lord Jesus, receive my spirit.' Then he knelt down and said aloud, 'Lord, do not hold this sin against them,' and with these words he fell asleep. Saul entirely approved of the killing.

(1st Reading of the 7th Sunday of Easter, Year C, with an extra verse.)

b. A reading from the letter of James   2: 14-18

Take the case, my brothers, of someone who has never done a single good act but claims that he has faith. Will that faith save him? If one of the brothers or one of the sisters is in need of clothes and has not enough food to live on, and one of you says to them, 'I wish you well; keep yourself warm and eat plenty,' without giving them these bare necessities of life, then what good is that? Faith is like that: if good works do not go with it, it is quite dead.

This is the way to talk to people of that kind: 'You say you have faith and I have good deeds; I will prove to you that I have faith by showing you my good deeds - now you prove to me that you have faith without any good deeds to show.'

(2nd Reading of the 24th Sunday in Ordinary Time, Year B)

c.   A reading from the book of the prophet Isaiah   6: 1-8

In the year of King Uzziah's death I saw the Lord seated on a high throne; his train filled the sanctuary; above him stood seraphs, each one with six wings.

> And they cried out one to another in this way,
> 'Holy, holy, holy is the Lord of hosts.
> His glory fills the whole earth.'

The foundations of the threshold shook with the voice of the one who cried out, and the Temple was filled with smoke. I said:

> 'What a wretched state I am in! I am lost,
> for I am a man of unclean lips
> and I live among a people of unclean lips,
> and my eyes have looked at the King, the Lord of hosts.'

Then one of the seraphs flew to me, holding in his hand a live coal which he had taken from the altar with a pair of tongs. With this he touched my mouth and said:

> 'See now, this has touched your lips,
> your sin is taken away,
> your iniquity is purged.'

Then I heard the voice of the Lord saying:

> 'Whom shall I send? Who will be our messenger?'

I answered, 'Here I am, send me.'

(1st Reading of the 5th Sunday in Ordinary Time, Year C)

7. Repetition and balance

Some passages in scripture contain a level of repetition that is unfamiliar to us today. The reader needs to find a way to deliver the message they contain without monotony. This can be achieved by emphasising the differences between the repetitive elements. Here is another situation when variation in voice pitch can help. Below are passages selected to illustrate this point and to provide opportunity for practice. It might be helpful to identify the particular problem before beginning to rehearse.

a.   A reading from the holy Gospel according to Matthew   5: 1-12

Seeing the crowds, he went up the hill. There he sat down and was joined by his disciples. Then he began to speak. This is what he taught them:

> 'How happy are the poor in spirit;
> theirs is the kingdom of heaven.
> Happy the gentle:
> they shall have the earth for their heritage.
> Happy those who mourn:

56

they shall be comforted.
Happy those who hunger and thirst for what is right:
they shall be satisfied.
Happy the merciful:
they shall have mercy shown them.
Happy the pure in heart:
they shall see God.
Happy the peacemakers:
they shall be called sons of God.
Happy those who are persecuted in the cause of right:
Theirs is the kingdom of heaven.

'Happy are you when people abuse you and persecute you and speak all kinds of calumny against you on my account. Rejoice and be glad, for your reward will be great in heaven.'

(4th Sunday in Ordinary Time, Year A; All Saints)

b. A reading from the holy Gospel according to Mark   13: 33-37

Jesus said to his disciples: 'Be on your guard, stay awake, because you never know when the time will come. It is like a man travelling abroad: he has gone from home, and left his servants in charge, each with his own task; and he has told the doorkeeper to stay awake. So stay awake, because you do not know when the master of the house is coming, evening, midnight, cockcrow, dawn; if he comes unexpectedly, he must not find you asleep. And what I say to you I say to all: Stay awake!'

(1st Sunday in Advent, Year B)

c. A reading from the book of the prophet Joel   2: 15-18

Sound the trumpet in Zion!
Order a fast,
proclaim a solemn assembly,
call the people together,
summon the community,
assemble the elders,
gather the children,
even the infants at the breast;
Let the bridegroom leave his bedroom,
and the bride her alcove.
Between vestibule and altar let the priests,
the ministers of the Lord, lament.

Let them say,
'Spare your people, Lord!
Do not make not your heritage a thing of shame,
a byword for the nations.
Why should it be said among the nations,
"Where is their God?" '

Then the Lord, jealous on behalf of his land,
took pity on his people.

(part of 1st Reading of Ash Wednesday)

d.   A reading from the first letter of John   4: 7-10

My dear people,
let us love one another
since love comes from God
and everyone who loves is begotten by God and knows God.
Anyone who fails to love can never have known God,
because God is love.
God's love for us was revealed
when God sent into the world his only Son
so that we could have life through him;
this is the love I mean:
not our love for God,
but God's love for us when he sent his Son
to be the sacrifice that takes our sins away.

(2nd Reading of the 6th Sunday of Easter, Year B)

APPENDIX C:

Samples of scripture commentaries

The purpose of this section is to give a flavour of the range and value of different commentaries at different levels. The range of titles used is not in any way exhaustive: understandably only a small selection can be given. But looking at the differences between them may help readers decide the kind of commentary or the range of commentaries that would be useful to the parish.

The extracts chosen refer to the Third Sunday of Lent, Year A, which has an unusually long bu t important Gospel reading.

Contents of Appendix B: 1: The First Reading; 2: The Second Reading (p.60); 3: The Gospel (p.61); 4: General Commentaries or on the Gospel only (p.65)

---

1. First reading: Exodus 17: 3-7

a. From *Sharing the Lectionary for Lent 2002: a Participant's Handbook*

THIS PASSAGE is the third in a series of tests. In the first test, the people doubted they would have water to drink (Ex 15: 22-27). In the second test, they doubted that they would have enough food (Ex 16: 1-36). Then again, at Meribah and Massah, they doubted that they would have water to drink.

The point of the passage is twofold. First, the Israelites were real people with real fears. They stepped out in faith to follow Moses into the desert, but when faced with a crisis, they failed to remember the protection God already had given them. They were afraid; their fear is expressed as anger – with Moses as the target. He reminds them of God's promises, and in an intimate confron-tation with God, Moses reminds God, too. The second and more important idea is that God *did* provide water for them. The essentials necessary for their journey were available to them.

The average rainfall in the southern Sinai is less than three inches per year. When rains come they are torrential. During these flash floods, water exerts great pressure on the walls of the canyons. Occasionally, water hollows great fissures inside the mountains that become reservoirs, holding thousands of gallons of water. After the flood, the water seeping from the reservoir forms calcium deposits that seal off the water in the rock. Bedouin shepherds, like Moses, know how to strike the rock in exactly the right place and break loose the blockage allowing the trea-sure of water to be revealed.

Though it would have been more pleasant to remember Meribah and Massah as places of great faith rather than great doubt, perhaps Israel itself needed the reminder that the people of the Exodus were not heroes, but human beings like us. Lack of faith, fear, anger, and mistrust are part of life's journey. God did not reject Israel; God gave Israel life through the water from the rock. Perhaps their greatness lies in their humility to tell a story about their doubt.

b. From *Workbook for Lectors and Gospel Readers 2002*, Aelred R. Rosser.

Today's readings are saturated with water imagery, especially this first reading and the gospel. Water is one of our most basic needs; life as we know it is impossible without water. How natural, then, that water initiates us into Christian life. It is through the water of baptism that we became who we are: members of the body of Christ and heirs of the reign of God.

It may be difficult for us today to appreciate the image of water, perhaps because for many of us water is taken for granted. It was not so with the Israelites during their sojourn in the desert, as indeed it is not for many people today, for whom water is a precious commodity. If we lived in one of the more arid parts of the world, like Palestine, we might be able to appreciate the readings today at a more elemental level.

In this first reading we witness a serious confrontation between Moses and the unruly people he is leading through the desert. They are panicky with thirst; Moses is frightened for his life. The real problem, of course, is that the people doubt that God will be with them in their need. Thus they ask a question that echoes in the heart of every believer who has undergone severe temptation or suffering: 'Is the Lord with us or not?'

The words Massah and Meribah mean 'quarrel' and 'testing,' as the text makes clear. You can indicate this by reading them with parallel emphasis. And don't shy away from the chilling question that ends the reading. It's a fact of life that we doubt and question, especially during the difficult times. This reading acknowledges our weakness and then demonstrates that the Lord does appear among us. Doubting is not a sin; it is part of the struggle inherent in a life of faith. We have a lot in common with the grumbling Israelites – our ancestors in faith – and we need not be ashamed of it.

c. From *Word and Worship Workbook for Year A*, Mary Birmingham

Today's reading refers to Israel's defining event: the exodus and the wanderings in the desert. Moses was instructed to strike the rock and water sprang forth. Water was a powerful symbol of God's activity. Water was a sign of life. At creation God hovered over the waters and breathed life into them. Water was a sign of destruction, purification, and God's awesome power. God sent down the rain for forty days and forty nights and submerged the earth because of the sin of human beings. Water was a sign of salvation. When the Israelites thirsted in the desert, water flowed through the power of God. In an arid land, water is an absolute need. Water is a symbol of liberation and passage from death to life. God held back the water for the Israelites to pass through.

Through the water sign there is allusion to the sacraments: water as salvation; water as sign of baptism. Lent is both penitential and baptismal in nature. The first reading touches on both themes.

The psalm for this liturgy exhorts us 'not to harden our hearts.' Meribah and Massah were the places where the people had sinned. This first reading reminds us of our total dependence on the God who saves, Christ who liberates, and the Spirit who leads us to the life-giving water.

2. Second reading: Romans 5: 1-2, 5-8

a. From *Workbook for Lectors and Gospel Readers 2002*

Christianity is not about what we are supposed to do. It is about what has already been done for us by a loving God. As obvious as this, it is difficult to live out in the practice of our faith. We have been justified by faith; we have been reconciled with God; we have been granted access to grace. Notice how all this is in the past tense. It has happened. It's a fact. It's a given. 'Have you been saved?' we are sometimes asked. Yes, we have. Have we accepted the salvation granted us out of pure love? Do we believe God loves us infinitely and without reserve? Well, there's the challenge. But the more we come to believe it, the more spontaneous and joyous our response to love will be. Good works are done not in the hope of earning God's favor – we already have that. Rather, good works express our gratitude.

To demonstrate his point, Paul illustrates the difference between human and divine love. Yes, on rare occasions we hear of one person giving up life itself out of love for another. Parents may sacrifice their own lives to save an endangered child, and they do so out of love for the child.

God's love for us in Christ is something like that, only greater. Christ died for us whether we deserved it or not. He died for us regardless of whether we care or not. He died for us whether or not we even hear about it until we meet him in glory! Perhaps most amazing is that in dying for us, he made us deserving. But he chose to leave us free to believe this good news or not. That, too, is a sign of his love and respect.

b. From *Word and Worship Workbook for Year A*

Up to this point in his letter to the Romans, Paul has expressed his assurance that human beings were justified through the redeeming death of Christ. Today's pericope is concerned with the implications of our justification. Since we are justified, we share the peace of Christ. Our faith in the paschal mystery gives us free access to God's grace as we wait in hope for our future glory. Paul reminds us that the Spirit continues to shower us with the living, ever-present love of God. Reginald Fuller maintains that Paul related justification to the indwelling of the Spirit. The Spirit of God initiates and continues the work of healing transformation within those the Spirit justifies. Each person is thus raised to a state of created grace. God pours out gratuitous love through the gift of the Spirit and through the sacrifice on the cross by God's Son, Jesus Christ. The veil of the curtain was torn at the death of Jesus and sinners were given access to God. That access is the Spirit of God. The gift of the cross is God's Holy Spirit dwelling within human beings to transform them into the elevated state they were destined to attain. We also hear in Paul's letter the roots of our belief in the Holy Trinity.

3. Gospel: John 4: 5-42

a. From *Sharing the Lectionary for Lent 2002: a Participant's Handbook*

The story of the woman at the well illustrates one person's acceptance of the gift of the Spirit and salvation. The acceptance of the water of faith, done in stages, moves the woman from sinner to disciple. Jesus engages the Samaritan woman at the well with a request for water. He is, like Israel, in need of water. He is vulnerable, tired and thirsty. As their conversation continues, she gradually expresses a fuller understanding of who Jesus is. At first, she addresses Jesus as a 'Jew' (v 9), and acts mistrustful. Why would Jesus, a Jew and a man, be speaking to her, a Samaritan and a woman?

Jesus asks her to recognize 'the gift of God' (v 10) and the water he offers her. Her next address, 'Sir' expresses more respect, but she misunder-stands the kind of water of which Jesus is speaking (a technique of many of John's stories). When she finally asks for the water, Jesus asks something of her: repentance. He is aware of her marital history.

The next level of her response is deeper. Because prophets often challenge people to repent, she now addresses Jesus as a prophet (v 19). She uses this occasion to resolve an age-old argument between the Samaritans and the Jews: just where are you supposed to worship (v 20)? Jesus' response is that the Jerusalem Temple is the spot, but pushes her beyond the Temple to a new kind of worship.

She then risks the next step, speaking of the Messiah (v 25). Jesus confirms her implied question by identifying himself as the one sent by God. Her final step is to become a disciple and evangelizer. She tells others in her village about Jesus (v 28). They in turn come to believe in Jesus, first on her testimony, and then because of their own encounter with 'his word' (v 41). The villagers are the representatives of the Christian community who first learn of Jesus from one of his followers and then who, through the encounter with the word (Gospel), come to believe on their own.

The water which Jesus thirsted for was the woman's faith. The woman gradually accepted the gift of living water from Jesus and shared that source of water with others. Though she is seemingly among the least likely to be a role model, this woman, a Samaritan and a sinner, provides a clear example of faith. Faith is a gift, gradually accepted. For those willing to accept it, it is the source of true life and refreshment, and the gateway to intimacy with God.

b. From *Workbook for Lectors and Gospel Readers 2002*

THE READINGS FOR THE Third, Fourth and Fifth Sundays of Lent this year (Year A) are so filled with basic images of our faith – water, light, death to life – that they may be read on those Sundays in Years B and C as well, in place of the readings proper to Years B and C. It is particularly fitting to exercise that option if there are catechumens in the assembly who are being prepared for reception into the church at the Easter Vigil. Next Sunday we hear about light in the story of the man born blind. On the Fifth Sunday of Lent we hear about life beyond death in the story of Lazarus, whom Jesus brought back from the dead.

Today we see the Israelites thirsting for water in the desert. Today we hear Paul tell us that the love of God has been 'poured out' into our hearts. And today we hear the story of the 'woman at the well,' a gospel story so popular and well known it has acquired this special title.

Taking the shorter form of this gospel weakens its impact, so avoid that if at all possible. If you are concerned about the celebration taking too long, consider other legitimate ways to abbreviate the liturgy. If you are worried that the assembly will find such a long reading boring, use your most accomplished deacon or priest to proclaim this text. Better yet, employ three readers and proclaim the gospel as we do the passion narratives on Palm Sunday and Good Friday. A narrator could read the narrative portions, along with the words of the disciples and the Samaritans. Another reader could proclaim the words of Jesus, and a third could proclaim the words of the woman. Such an approach will not only avert boredom, it will also bring a new life to the story. It goes without saying, I hope, that the three readers should spend considerable time and effort preparing!

Begin your study of this gospel by reminding yourself that, in the words of the gospel writer, 'Jews have nothing to do with Samaritans.' Then notice as you approach the end of the story that the Samaritans come to Jesus and beg him to stay with them awhile.

While these startling expressions of reconciliation between groups known for their mutual hatred are not the central point of John's account, they colour it from start to finish. You might recall as well that Jesus is breaking another taboo by speaking with a woman in public, and a Samaritan woman at that. It's not a bad thing to keep in mind the reconciling power of Jesus' presence as we hear him, tired from his journey, ask for a drink of water and then reveal himself as the Messiah. Only one other time do we hear Jesus speak of his thirst – when he was lifted up on the cross and drew all the world to himself.

Though the story centres on water and its many associations, there are many other instances that urge us to look for the deeper meaning in the several topics raised in this encounter between Jesus and the Samaritan woman. The woman speaks of water, and Jesus turns the conversation to living water. The woman refers to Jacob, giver of the well, the source of the water, and Jesus makes it clear that indeed he is greater than Jacob. Jesus has a different kind of water to offer. The woman brings up the disagreement about where one should worship God, and Jesus explains that God is Spirit and can be worshipped anywhere by one with a truthful heart.

Even the disciples provide Jesus with an opportunity to speak of deeper matters. They urge him to eat something. He speaks of bringing the Father's work to completion as the food that sustains him. Finally, Jesus speaks of the gratuitous gift of God, Jesus himself. There is no need to sow, for the harvest is provided. God has done the work, and we reap the grain without labour. God has become one with us: 'Sower and reaper may rejoice together.'

A sensitive proclamation should concentrate on revealing as much of the richness here as possible. The vivid imagery, the rich dialogue, the underlying issues of race and gender, the questions of the disciples and the conversion of the Samaritans make this gospel story one of the most formative, educational, and inspiring of the New Testament.

c. From *Word and Worship Workbook for Year A*

THE EXEGESIS FOR THE GOSPEL of the Samaritan woman at the well will utilize the insights of Sandra Schneider, a biblical scholar. In my opinion, her interpretation most thoroughly uncovers the heart and soul, not only of the text, but of its place in baptismal and lenten catechesis. At a recent workshop, Donald Senior, one of this country's (US) most respected biblical scholars, asserted that the scholarly work of Schneider in relation to this gospel is masterful and right on the mark. He was surprised that no one had stumbled across it before. He surmised that it was because most biblical scholars have been male. As male members of the community, they approach the texts primarily with a masculine hermeneutic *(i.e: interpretation)*. Biblical texts are to be interpreted not only through the science of biblical criticism, but also through the discerning wisdom of the community. For most of its history, the church has not had the privilege of the discernment of half of her members – the female half.[19] The scholar further noted that the feminine consciousness has not had the opportunity to interpret the texts. That is presently changing with the emergence of many female biblical scholars.

Schneider approaches the text with an attitude of suspicion.[20] She confronts the story, suspicious of its obvious moral dilemma: a woman chastised for her sexual indiscretions. It appears as though Schneider sidesteps the patriarchal literal meaning, turning instead to the images, symbols, and typology common to the time and to the Johannine community, in order to appropriate a more inclusive interpretation.

Some scholars suggest that the story of the Samaritan woman probably was not an historical story. The story served as legitimization of the Samaritan mission in John's community; to establish full equality between Samaritan and Jewish Christians, and to affirm Jewish legitimacy as bearer of covenant faith but with a surprising recognition of the essential validity of Samaritan faith and inclusion in the covenant.[21]

Samaria was a territory north of Jerusalem. It was part of the Assyrian and Persian empire in 721-612 BCE. The Assyrians imported foreign colonists and deported many of Samaria's native citizens; others sought refuge in Judea. A Yahwism* influenced by other religions developed that led to animosity from traditional Jews. The bad feeling between the two groups was further exacerbated when the Samaritans offered to help rebuild the temple after the exile and were turned down by their Jewish brothers and sisters.

This added fuel to the already smouldering fires of resentment. Another revolt forced the Samaritans to move to Shechem where they built a temple on Mount Gerizim.[22] Samaritans anticipated a pro-phet like Moses who would restore worship on Mount Gerizim in northern Israel. The Jews, on the other hand, believed the messiah would be a descendant of David who would restore worship in the Jerusalem temple. It was obvious that resent-ments ran deep and permeated the consciousness of the two peoples. They were bitter enemies.

In the story of the Samaritan woman, it is the unspoken text between the lines that captures our attention and imagination. The woman is nameless. Nameless people in scripture often represent more than the literal eye can see, especially in John's gospel (the beloved disciple, the royal official, the paralytic at the pool, and the man born blind). This woman is a symbolic figure who represents the Samaritan people and the New Israel (the new kingdom).

The woman was at a well – not just any well, but a famous well. Wells were important symbolic places in biblical literature. Important events in salvation history began with unions initiated at famous wells. Rebecca was found for Isaac at a well; Rachel met Jacob at the very well in this story. Before this scene in John's gospel, at the wedding in Cana, Jesus was called the new Bridegroom. Our attention in this reading, then, turns to Jesus, the new Bridegroom, present at the well of famous weddings to 'claim Samaria as beloved in the New Israel'.[23]

There is more to consider about the heroine of the story. She was a woman and a Samaritan, the lowest on society's totem pole. Even the pagans hated Samaritans. She was an outcast's outcast! Yet this outcast, woman and Samaritan, en-countered Christ. Jesus, a Jew, not only spoke to her and noticed her, but he drank from her bucket (making him ritually unclean). The woman was trained by her culture to believe she was worthless. Yet this Jew offered her acceptance, dignity, com-passion, a way out, and a way in! Donald Senior suggests that this woman has much more to teach us than a lesson on morality. It is the story between the lines we dare to hear.

During the exile the Samaritans remained faithful to Yahweh, but became inculturated by their conquerors.

---

* **Yahwism: worship of the God who revealed his name as Yahweh to Moses, as opposed to worship of another named God or of many gods**

While they still loved Yahweh, they nevertheless dabbled in the local worship of the Samaritan gods. The result was that Jews hated the Samaritans whom they judged unfaithful. Samaritans were outcasts and ritually unclean. No good Jew would drink from this woman's bucket. Yet Jesus drank from her bucket. In his encounter with her, Jesus welcomed the lost and included the sinner, the outsider.

She entered into a theological discussion with him. She interrogated him about his action toward her. He had broken Jewish tradition by speaking to her (a woman) and by using the same utensils she had used. She was dumbfounded. Samaritans would have been shocked to hear anyone claiming to be on the same plane as their patriarch Jacob who had given the well to Israel in the first place. Jesus acknowledged Samaria's rightful place in salvation history while still affirming Yahweh's convenant with the Jews. Yet he made it very clear that they had each missed the boat – both the Jews and the Samaritans. Neither had a monopoly on the truth. God was doing something new. While defending the Jewish claim to the covenant tradition, Jesus made no distinction regarding the *territory* people worshiped in. what was important was the worship Jesus would inaugurate as messiah – worship in spirit and truth, authentic worship. The gospel would guide the worship. In the new kingdom people would live in biblical justice, in right relationship with God. They would live the law of love.

Centred in the middle of Jesus' theological discussion with the woman is his scrutiny of her adulterous liaisons – her five husbands. That she had had five husbands was unusual in the religious society of her day. 'Either this is totally out of place, a trivial bit of moralism or even a shallow display of preternatural knowledge on the part of Jesus, or it is an integral part of this highly theological exchange."[24] This story is about the *inclusion* of Samaria into the New Israel. Jesus scrutinized the woman's (Samaria's) adulterous (idolatrous) union with the gods of the five tribes. 'Jesus' declaration that Samaria "has no husband" is a classic prophetic denunciation of false worship, like Hosea's oracle in which the prophet expresses God's sentiment toward unfaithful Israel' (Hos 2: 2).[25] Thus, Jesus suggests that Samaria's relationship to Yahweh in the past was colored by her adulterous flirtations with other gods. Jesus scrutinized the false worship, named the sin, and invited repentance as he included Samaria in his New Israel.

At this wedding well, in broad daylight and at high noon so that all could see, Jesus, the new *Bridegroom*, wed Samaria and included her in the kingdom.[26] 'Now the new Bridegroom who assumed the role of Yahweh, bridgroom of ancient Israel, comes to claim Samaria as an integral part of the New Israel, namely, the Christian community and specifically the Johannine community'.[27]

What, then, was the woman's response? She recognized Jesus for who he was, messiah and lord. She could do no less than 'go and tell everyone... and they all came to believe on her testimony.' She was the first evangelist and the only person to bring an entire group of people to faith in Jesus. No wonder women had an important ministerial role in John's community.[28]

The implications? Jesus extended reconciliation, inclusion, and healing to alienated Samaria; everyone is included in the reign of God. Jesus shared this revelation with a woman – society's outcast (then and in many places today).[29] He treated her as he would have treated any member of his society – with respect and dignity. We are, by extension, invited to cast aside any idols of our making that get in the way of our authentic worship of God, and we are to welcome all who are on the bottom rung of society.

This is a story about the kingdom in which there are no outcasts and no strangers, only repentant, welcomed sinners. 'In summary, the entire dialogue between Jesus and the woman is the "wooing" of Samaria to full covenant fidelity in the New Israel by Jesus, the New Bridegroom. It has nothing to do with the woman's private moral life, but with the covenant life of the community. Nowhere in the fourth gospel is there a dialogue of such theological depth and intensity.'[30]

In light of the celebration of the scrutinies, this gospel helps us name the social and personal sin that keeps us from an intimate relationship with God. We are reminded that it is God who names our sin, who scrutinizes the evil in our lives, and who invites us to turn away from anything (our personal and corporate idols) that keeps us from a full liberated life in Christ. Today's liturgy highlights the evil of exclusion on any level: in our personal lives, in our society, and in our religious structures. It demands that we ask the questions: *Who is out?* and *Who is in?* Like the woman, we are to go out and invite others in. today's gospel invites *metanoia* – a complete turning away *from* sin *toward* the Healer, Liberator, Victor, and One who offers living water through the refreshing waters of baptism. This is the victory Christ holds out to us in today's liturgy.

4. General commentaries on all of the readings or on the gospel only

a. From *Let the Scriptures Speak: Reflections on the Sunday Readings* (Dennis Hamm, S.J.)

What we thirst for

ABOUT TEN YEARS AGO, I heard a Samaritan scholar (one of the five hundred or so Samaritans alive on planet Earth) address an audience at the local Jewish community centre. I was stunned when he told those assembled, 'We Samaritans and you Jews are both heirs of the ancient Israelite tradition. But the Torah says nothing about centering worship in Jerusalem. In Deuteronomy, God says to worship 'in the place where I will cause my name to dwell.' We know where that place is, Schechem, at Mount Gerizim, where Joshua first set up an altar. So we Samaritans are the authentic exponents of the Israelite tradition. You Jews are the heretics to the south.' I was shocked. But the mainly Jewish audience around me did not seem disturbed. After some twenty-seven hundred years of shared history, they knew perfectly well what Samaritans thought about the right place to worship God. So they were not surprised. For me, the remark was a vivid reminder of the background that underlies part of the dialogue between Jesus and the woman at the well in this Sunday's Gospel.

The topic of Samaritans and Jews leads naturally to thoughts about what divides and what unites human beings generally. And today's Gospel story centres around what we have most in common – thirst for God. The perfect symbol for the thirst for God is our common thirst for water. Next to carbon, the thing that all life forms we know about have most in common is water. We human beings begin our early development floating in the amniotic fluid of our mother's womb. Once out of that sea-like environment, our bodies insist that we continue to imbibe water, first in our mother's milk, then wherever we can find it, all the days of our lives.

One of the best places on earth to get in touch with this human need for water is Israel and the Occupied Territories. For there fresh water sources are scarce, and the precious rainwater that falls during the winter must be captured and kep in cisterns for use during the dry part of the year. Since water held in cisterns can get stale and contaminated, people came to call the fresh water of spring-fed sources 'living water,' to distinguish it from the relatively 'dead' water kept in cisterns. In

that setting, it is easy to understand how water, especially 'living water,' came to be a powerful metaphor for God's relationship with human beings. Take, for example, Jeremiah's words:

> Two evils have my people done:
> they have forsaken me, the source of living water;
> They have dug themselves cisterns,
> broken cisterns, that hold no water (Jer 2: 13).

One of the tourist sites in the Holy Land with the best claim to authenticity is the well at Nablus (near ancient Shechem/Sychar). It is the only well of spring-fed water in the area, and it is likely thousands of years old.

All of this water talk helps us to follow the dialogue between Jesus and the Samaritan woman. When the Samaritan woman rebuffs Jesus' request for a drink, he says if she knew the gift of God and who was making the request, she would have asked him, and he would have given her *living water*. As so often happens in the Fourth Gospel, Jesus' interlocutor misunderstands, and takes literally ('living water' = spring-fed water) what he means figuratively ('living water' = the gift of the Holy Spirit, a meaning that is hinted here but becomes clear in John 7: 37-39).

When the woman refers to the ancient sore point between Jews and Samaritans about the right place to worship (Jerusalem or Mount Gerizim), Jesus says, 'The hour is coming, and is now here, when true worshippers will worship the Father in spirit and truth.... God is Spirit, and those who worship him must worship in spirit and truth.' This encounter prompts the woman to abandon her jar and proceed to evangelize her village, who come to believe that Jesus is 'the saviour of the world.'

This passage speaks powerfully to our project of evangelization today. It reminds us that the Good News of God in Jesus is meant to overcome ancient hostilities and cross-cultural barriers. Though its source is concrete and specific ('salvation is from the Jews' – John 4:22), the gift of God in Jesus is meant for all who thirst for God. Jesus is the saviour of the world.

b. From *Reading the Gospels with the Church from Christmas through Easter* (Raymond E. Brown, S.S.)

Lenten Stories from John's Gospel: Water, Light and Life

FOR MANY CENTURIES, dating back to the ancient Jerusalem liturgy, the Church has singled out stories from John's Gospel to be read at Mass during Lent. In our era, three of these stories – the most sacred *narratives* in the Gospel accounts of Jesus' public ministry – appear on the third, fourth and fifth Sundays of Lent. They are the Samaritan woman at the well (John 4), the healing of the man born blind (John 9) and the raising of Lazarus (John 11).

These three accounts are so important liturgically that the Church grants permission for them to be read not only in the assigned year of the liturgical cycle A (1996, 1999, 2002), but in the second and third years (B, C) as well, so that there may never be a Lent in which they are not proclaimed.

Why are these stories given such prominence during Lent? Because during this season, from the earliest days, people were being prepared for Baptism, and John's stories fitted beautifully into the process of Christian initiation. In time, the three narratives were read at specific stages in the Lenten preparation of catechumens for Baptism on Holy Saturday. And as we shall see, they still serve admirably in reflecting on the implications of our own baptismal faith. To get the most from the discussion, keep your missal or New Testament nearby so you can follow the stories in their entirety.

John's Narrative Skill

The particular genius of John's Gospel is the use of clever dramatic devices that pull readers or hearers into the action. Unlike the Gospels of Matthew, Mark and Luke, which tend to offer *brief* scenes in describing Jesus' public ministry, the Gospel of John provides lengthy encounters in which we can see how the people react to Jesus and grow in faith.

John's narratives thus lend themselves to liturgical usage. John even supplies directions for dramatization so that any of the three long stories read in Lent can easily be staged. For instance, in a double-camera technique John tells us what the Samaritan woman is saying to the villagers on the side stage while the main attention is focused on center stage where Jesus speaks to his disciples (John 4: 27-39)

John wants 'you' to get engaged. The dramatic technique of John's Gospel matches its theology. Near the end of his Gospel, the evangelist states that the reason for his writing is that '*you* may believe that Jesus is the Messiah, the Son of God, and that through this belief you may have life in his name' (20: 31). The evangelist is reaching out to 'you' on the principle that everyone in every time and place must encounter Jesus in order to have life.

The characters described as encountering Jesus in the Gospel (the Samaritan woman, the man born blind, Martha and Mary) are in a way Everyman and Everywoman. Their encounters are narrated for your sake so that in them you may recognize yourself and be drawn into meeting Jesus in your life.

John wants us to move beyond this world. The encounter is not easy, for in John's theology Jesus has come from another world in order to reveal realities beyond human experience – realities that John calls 'true' or 'genuine.' Yet because the Word 'from above" has become flesh, the only language in which he can express his revelation is human language, the language 'from below.'

That can lead to confusion. For instance, Jesus speaks of water (to the Samaritan woman), sight (in reference to the blind man) and life (in the story of Lazarus); and those who encounter him think of well-known earthly concerns. In reality, however, Jesus is not speaking of earthly water that we drink only to get thirsty again, but of water that springs up to eternal life. He is not referring to the physical sight that people can possess without being able to perceive anything they cannot touch, but to a sight into heavenly realities. He is not simply renewing a life that ends in the grave, but offering a life whereby one does not die at all.

In John's stories, then, there is a constant double level of language. Those who talk to Jesus or about him speak of what is important to them on one level (earth) while Jesus tries to lead them to another, more important level of realities (heaven). By reading these stories to us in the liturgy, the Church reminds us that Jesus is still struggling to get us to see deeper realities.

The symbols of water, sight and new life are symbols closely associated with Christian Baptism and so, as we shall discover, the stories centered on them lead us to reflect on our baptismal faith, whether we are candidates for Baptism or have already been baptized.

The Woman at the Well: Coming to Faith and Living Water

This first story (John 4: 1-42) illustrates how difficult it is to come to Jesus in faith because of the various obstacles that stand in the way. If I were freely composing a story of conversion, I might imagine a central character eager to receive God. John is more realistic: Many people have a chip on their shoulder in regard to God because they feel beaten down by the inequalities in life. The woman smarts from the Jewish dislike for Samaritans, especially for Samaritan women. And that is her first obstacle to dealing with Jesus. 'How can you, a Jew,' she comments sarcastically, 'ask me, a Samaritan woman, for a drink?'

Jesus does not answer her objection; he is not going to change instantly a whole world of injustice. Yet he can offer something that will enable the woman to put injustice in perspective, namely, living water. He means water that gives life; she mis-understands it as flowing, bubbling water, con-temptuously asking him if he thinks he is greater than Jacob, who provided a well. (Is not 'No thanks – I already have all I need' our first reaction when someone tries to interest us in something new religiously?)

Ironically, as John expects the reader to recognize, Jesus is greater than Jacob; but again Jesus refuses to be sidetracked from his main goal. Accordingly, he explains that he is speaking of the water that springs up to eternal life, a water that will permanently end thirst. With masterful touch John shows the woman attracted on a level of the convenience of not having to come to the well every day for water. (People are not so different today: many are attracted to the message of those media evangelists who promote a religion that makes life more comfortable.)

To move the woman to a higher level, Jesus shifts the focus to her husband. Her reply is a half-truth, but Jesus shows that he is aware of her five husbands and of the live-in who is not her husband.

Today also, a far from perfect past is not an uncommon obstacle to conversion. To be brought to faith people must acknowledge where they stand, but they can take hope from the fact that Jesus persists even though he knows the woman's state. He does not say to the woman, 'Come back after you straighten out your life,' for the grace that he offers is meant to help her to change.

The Messiah is here! Confronted with Jesus' surprising knowledge of her situation, the woman seeks to take advantage of the fact that he is obviously a religious figure. Her question about whether to worship in the Jerusalem Temple or on Mount Gerizim is a typical ploy designed to distract. When is the last time she worried about such theological differences? Even today when we encounter someone who probes our lives, we are often adept at bringing up as a distraction some old religious chestnut, so as to avoid making a decision.

Once more Jesus refuses to be sidetracked. Although salvation is from the Jews, a time is coming and is now here when such an issue is irrelevant: Cult at both sites will be replaced by worship in Spirit and truth. Nimbly the woman tries one more ploy by shifting any decision to the distant future when the Messiah comes, but Jesus will not let her escape. His 'I am he' confronts her with a current demand for faith.

The disciples, too, must dig deeper. What follows, enacted dramatically on two stages, reveals even more about faith. In centre stage we observe that the disciples, who have now been with Jesus some time, understand his heavenly symbolism no better than the woman who encountered him for the first time. When he speaks of the food that he already has to eat, they wonder if someone has brought him a sandwich! Jesus has to explain: 'My food is to do the will of the One who sent me…' (John 4: 34)

On the side stage, we find that the woman is still not fully convinced since she poses to the villagers the question, 'Could this be the Messiah?' The villagers come and encounter Jesus for themselves so that their faith is not simply dependent on her account but on personal contact. We are left to surmise that by being instrumental in bringing others to believe, the woman's own faith came to completion. And at last she drank of the water of life.

c. From *The Cultural World of Jesus, Cycle A* (John J. Pilch)

A POPULAR PROVERB says: 'Familiarity breeds contempt.' In the case of Bible stories, familiarity blunts sensitivity and often blocks proper understanding. Anyone familiar with Mediterranean culture immediately identifies shocking and jarring elements in this story.

What is wrong with this picture?

Scholars doubt that this event ever took place in the life of Jesus. There is no Synoptic evidence for a ministry in Samaria. Indeed, Jesus forbade it (Matt 10:5). After the resurrection, John was involved in the mission to Samaria (Acts 8: 1-8), and the Johannine community contained Samaritan believers. This scene was, therefore, likely read back into Jesus' lifetime from the history of the Johannine community.

From a Mediterranean cultural perspective, there are other irregularities that offer new insight into the story.

(1) Wrong place, wrong time. The Mediterranean world is divided according to gender. Women have their places (kitchen, home); men have theirs (outdoors, the fields, the gate, the marketplace). The well is space common to both men and women, but they ought not to be there at the same time. Women can use the place only in the morning or evening. Here, the woman comes to the well at noon (v 6). Wrong time, and therefore wrong place.

Likely she comes at this hour because the women of her village shun her for her shameless behaviour (five husbands, now living with someone other than her husband, vv 16-18). She comes to the well at an hour when other women will be properly elsewhere. She is alone.

(2) Speaking to a strange man in public. Even the woman admits this irregularity. 'How is it that you, a Judean man, ask me, a Samaritan woman, for a drink?' (v 9) Culture indicates that the problem is not different ethnic heritage but different genders. For a man to speak to an unchaperoned woman in a public place is very suspicious. The disciples take note and are shocked! They did not dare to ask the obvious cultural questions: 'What do you want from her?' or 'Why are you talking to her?' (v 27)

(3) Talking to other men in a public place. After her discussion with and enlightenment by Jesus, the woman went to the village marketplace, the place reserved for men; women should not enter there when men are present. And she admits to them that Jesus knew what they all knew: that she was a shameless woman, who behaved shamelessly regarding cultural rules governing proper behaviour between men and women (notably marriage).

What is the evangelist intending to say with this scene?

Clearly, a cultural subversion is taking place. Modern social scientists would call this a cultural innovation. John seems to be confirming new roles for women in his community.

Jesus not only talks with the woman, but in a carefully orchestrated, seven-part dialogue (each speaks seven times) he guides her progressively from ignorance to enlightenment, from misunderstanding to clearer understanding. She is the most carefully and intensely catechized person in this entire Gospel!

Though the woman demonstrates her brazenness in discussing 'masculine,' political-religious topics ('Messiah' and 'Temple') with Jesus, he accepts her questions and answers them rather than steering her back to 'feminine' topics. Revolutionary, indeed!

Some scholars go so far as to claim that this mixed-breed woman is the first disciple in John's Gospel. They suggest that Jesus himself commissioned her when he said: 'Go call your husband, and come back' (v 16).

Others disagree and note the following con-trast. The evangelist reports: 'Many Samaritans from that city believed in Jesus because of the woman's testimony' (v 39). But the village men in the narrative offer a left-handed compliment: 'It is no longer because of what you said that we believe, for we have heard for ourselves' (v 42).

Comparing and contrasting women's place in ancient Mediterranean and contemporary Western culture is instructive in its own right but ought not deflect attention from the woman's astonishing and rapid insight into who Jesus really is: 'Judaean (a scornfully pronounced identification)', 'sir', 'prophet', and 'Messiah', leading ultimately to the village's recognition of Jesus as 'Saviour of the world.' Would that all believers could progress as insightfully and rapidly as she and her village.

READING LIST

The following titles have been used in the preparation and conduct of the course, many of which are considered useful additions to a parish library. ISBNs (International Standard Book Numbers) are quoted as they are sometimes asked for when ordering the books.

Birmingham, Mary, *Word & Worship Workbook for Year A, for Ministry in Initiation, Preaching, Religious Education and Formation,* Paulist Press, 1999 (ISBN 0-8091-3826-3), Year B, Paulist Press 2000 (0-8091-3898-0), Year C, Paulist Press 1998 (I0-8-91-3747-X)

Boadt, Lawrence, *Reading the Old Testament: An Introduction*, Paulist Press 1984 (0-8091-2631-1)

Bonneau, Normand, OMI, *Preparing the Table of the Word,* The Liturgical Press, 1997 (0-8146-2499-5)

Charpentier, Etienne, *How to Read the Old Testament,* SCM Press Ltd, 1982 (0-334-02056-5)

--------*How to Read the New Testament*, SCM Press Ltd, 1982 (0-334-02057-3)

Hamm, Dennis, *Let the Scriptures Speak: Reflections on the Sunday Readings, Year A*, The Liturgical Press, 2001 (ISBN Year B: 0-8146-2556-8)

Harrington, Donal and Julie Kavanagh, *Prayer for Parish Groups: preparing and leading prayer for group meetings*, Columba, 1998 (1-85607-241-X)

Lonergan, Ray, *A Well-trained Tongue, a workbook for Lectors,* Liturgy Training Publications, 1982 (0-930467-39-6)

Myers, Susan E, *Pronunciation Guide for the Sunday Lectionary*, Liturgy Training Publications, 1998 (1-56854-297-6)

Perkins, Pheme, *Reading the New Testament: An Introduction*, Paulist Press, revised edition 1988 (0-8091-2939-6)

Philipps, James, *Unlocking the Treasures of the Bible: A Practical Guide*, Twenty-Third Publications 2002 (1-58595-2228-1

Ralph, Margaret Nutting, *And God Said What?: An Introduction to Biblical Literary Forms*, Paulist Press, Revised 2003 (0-8091-4129-0)

Reid, Barbara E, *Parables for Preachers,* The Liturgical Press, 2001. Year A: 0-8146-2550-9; Yr B: 0-8146-2551-7; Yr C: 0-8146-2552-5

Rosser, Aelred R, *Workbook for Lectors and Gospel Readers*, Year B, 2003, Liturgy Training publications, 2002 (ISBN – USA – 1-56854-402-2)

Scagnelli, Peter J, *Sourcebook for Sundays and Seasons: An Almanac of Parish Liturgy*, 2000, Year B, Liturgy Training Publications, 1998 (1-56854-293-3)

Tolley, Marian, *A Handbook for Readers: A practical and liturgical guide*, Decani Books 2001 (ISBN 1-9003-1412-6)

Zimmerman, Joyce Ann, C.P.P.S., et al, *Living Liturgy: Spirituality, Celebration, and Cathechesis,* The Liturgical Press, 2001. Year A: 0-8146-2569-X; Yr B: 0-8146-2567-3; Yr C: 0-8146-2568-1

Special mention needs to be made of the series *Sacra Pagina,* edited by Daniel J. Harrington, S.J., and published by The Columba Press. There are currently fifteen titles in the series, providing commentary on all the books of the New Testament. A similar series, called *Berit Olam,* offers the latest in literary analysis of the volumes of the Old Testament.

There are many titles addressed to preachers of the Word which will be of use to all who wish to understand scripture better. Those interested should consult the catalogue of The Columba Press.

Where to obtain these books

All the titles above are available through one or the other of: St Paul's Multimedia Centres in all major cities, Decani, or McCrimmons (for Liturgy Training Publications).

FOOTNOTES

[1] Normand Bonneau, OMI, *Preparing the Table of the Word*, The Liturgical Press, 1997, p 8.

[2] Joe Paprocki, God's Library: Introducing Catholics to the Bible, *Twenty-Third Publications*, 1999, p 9.

[3] Jean Marie Hiesberger, General Editor, The Catholic Bible, Personal Study Edition, OUP, 1995.

[4] Etienne Charpentier, How to read the Old Testament, SCM Press, 1982, p 25.

[5] CSL 51

[6] from Godfrey Diekmann, O.S.B.: source not identified

[7] Whether the passage is from the Old Testament or the New, the reader introduces it by saying only 'A reading from…' There is no need to refer to first reading or second reading: we have been doing this for more than forty years now and the assembly knows which reading is which.

[8] From Ray Longergan, *A Workbook for Lectors: A well-trained tongue*, Liturgy Training Publications, 1982, p 25.

[9] Ibid, p 19.

[10] Richard J Clifford, SJ, 'Psalms' in the *Collegeville Bible Commentary: Old Testament*, p 754.

[11] Carroll Stuhlmueller, CP, 'An Introduction to the Book of Psalms', *Psalms for Morning and Evening Prayer*, Liturgy Training Publications.

[12] The Grail Psalms translated from the Hebrew, Collins, p 9.

[13] Ibid, p 10.

[14] Ibid, p 5.

[15] *General Introduction to the Lectionary*, 123.

[16] Apocalypse 1: 9.

[17] Pheme Perkins in *The Collegeville Bible Commentary based on the New American Bible:* New Testament, The Liturgical Press, 1992, p 1267.

[18] Ibid, p 1269.

[19] Barbara Reid, in her book, *Choosing the Better Part* (Collegeville: The Liturgical Press, 1996), describes the vision that best informs the exegesis for this liturgy. 'Patriarchy is "any system, organization, or institution in which the men own, administer, shape, or control a major portion of all the facet of society.' (Joan Chittister, Yesterday's *Dangerous Vision: Christian Feminism in the Catholic Church*, in *Sojourners* (July 1987): 18) The world of Jesus was a patriarchal world, as is our own, although that is beginning to change. Feminism, as a response to patriarchy, 'is a commitment to the humanity, dignity, and equality of all persons to such a degree that one is willing to work for changes in structures and in relationship patterns so that these occur to the equal good of all' (Chittister, 18)… Feminism advocates a community of equals that provides for all the members, women and men alike, to use their God-given gifts to the benefit of all. Christian feminists are women and men committed to eliminating sexism in their relations with one another, in the structures of their faith communities and in society. They see this as a work of justice that is truly faithful to the teaching and life of Jesus…" (Reid, 7)

[20] '…A hermeneutic of suspicion recognizes that the biblical texts have been written, for the most part, by men, for men, and about men, and that they serve the interests of patriarchy. One who reads with a hermeneutic of suspicion is wary that the text can be oppressive for women. This does not deny the inspiration of Scripture, but recognizes the limitations of the human authors that set forth God's word.' (Reid, 9)

[21] Dunning, Jim, *Echoing God's Word*, 306.

[22] For further information, refer to: Robert F O'Toole, SJ, 'Samaria/Samaritan,' in Stuhlmueller, Carroll, C.P., ed. *The Collegeville Pastoral Dictionary of Biblical Theology*, 872-873.

[23] Dunning, Jim, *Echoing God's Word*, 306.

[24] Schneiders, Sandra, *The Revelatory Text*, 190.

[25] Ibid.

[26] Contrast the woman coming to the well at high noon, in the light of day for all to see, with Nico-demus, who came in the dead of night. John's gospel is filled with the metaphor of night and day, light and darkness.

[27] Schneiders, 187.

[28] See Sixteenth Sunday in Ordinary Time: the story of Martha and Mary.

[29] At the time of Christ, in order for something to be attested and affirmed, it had to be verified in a court of law. I find it very interesting that first-hand testimony and events often occurred to people who could not legally witness to them in the courts. Women could not serve as verifiable witnesses unless the issue pertained to a household matter. Shepherds were also not allowed to testify as valid witnesses, since they were considered too untrustworthy to give truthful testimony. Yet, is it not God's irony (or perhaps humour) that the two premier events of redemptive salvation were witnessed by people who, by human standards, were not able to verify or testify to what they had witnessed? Shepherds were the first to witness the Incarnation and a woman was first on the scene following the resurrection. Once again, God writes salvation history with crooked lines and refuses to be boxed in by humanity's standards of convention. In today's story, a woman experienced the messiah. Her experience and her story alone had the power to invite people to faith.

[30] Schneiders, 191.